Hmong

IN MINNESOTA

Chia Youyee Vang

Foreword by Bill Holm

M MINNESOTA HISTORICAL SOCIETY PRESS

Cover: Decorative coins, photo by Shia Yang; Hmong children, courtesy May A Yang

Publication of this book was supported, in part, with funds provided by the June D. Holmquist Publication Endowment Fund of the Minnesota Historical Society.

www.mhspress.org

The Minnesota Historical Society Press is a member of the Association of American University Presses.

Manufactured in Canada

10 9 8 7 6 5 4 3 2 1

♾ The paper used in this publication meets the minimum requirements of the American National Standard for Information Sciences—Permanence for Printed Library Materials, ANSI Z39.48–1984.

International Standard Book Number 10: 0-87351-598-6 (paper)
International Standard Book Number 13: 978-0-87351-598-6 (paper)

Library of Congress Cataloging-in-Publication Data

Vang, Chia Youyee, 1971–
    Hmong in Minnesota / Chia Youyee Vang ; foreword by Bill Holm.
       p.   cm. — (The people of Minnesota)
    Includes bibliographical references and index.
    ISBN-13: 978-0-87351-598-6 (paper : alk. paper)
    ISBN-10: 0-87351-598-6 (paper : alk. paper)
       1. Hmong Americans—Minnesota—History. 2. Refugees—Minnesota—History.
    3. Immigrants—Minnesota—History. 4. Hmong Americans—Minnesota—
    Social conditions. 5. Hmong Americans—Minnesota—Social life and customs.
    6. Minnesota—Ethnic relations. I. Title.

F615.H55V36 2008
977.6'00495972—dc22

                                                                              2007032459

This book was designed and set in type by Wendy Holdman, Stanton Publication Services, Minneapolis, Minnesota; it was printed by Friesens, Altona, Manitoba.

Contents

Foreword

by Bill Holm

Human beings have not been clever students at learning any lessons from their three or four thousand odd years of recorded history. We repeat our mistakes from generation to generation with tedious regularity. But we ought to have learned at least one simple truth: that there is no word, no idea that is not a double-edged sword. Take, for example, the adjective *ethnic.* In one direction, it cuts upward, to show us the faces, the lives, the histories of our neighbors and ourselves. It shows us that we are not alone on this planet—that we are all rooted with deep tendrils growing down to our ancestors and the stories of how they came to be not *there,* but *here.* These tendrils are visible in our noses and cheekbones, our middle-aged diseases and discomforts, our food, our religious habits, our celebrations, our manner of grieving, our very names. The fact that here in Minnesota, at any rate, we mostly live together in civil harmony— showing sometimes affectionate curiosity, sometimes puzzled irritation but seldom murderous violence—speaks well for our progress as a community of neighbors, even as members of a civilized human tribe.

But early in this new century in America we have seen the dark blade of the ethnic sword made visible, and it has cut us to the quick. From at least one angle, our national wounds from terrorist attacks are an example of ethnicity gone mad, tribal loyalty whipped to fanatical hysteria, until it turns human beings into monstrous machines of mass murder. Few tribes own a guiltless history in this regard.

The twentieth century did not see much progress toward solving the problem of ethnicity. Think of Turk and Armenian, German and Jew, Hutu and Tutsi, Protestant and Catholic, Albanian and Serb, French and Algerian—think of our own lynchings. We all hoped for better from the twenty-first century but may not get any reprieve at all from the tidal waves of violence and hatred.

As global capitalism breaks down the borders between nation-states, fanatical ethnicity rises to life like a hydra. Cheerful advertisements assure us that we are all a family—wearing the same pants, drinking the same pop, singing and going online together as we spend. When we invoke *family,* we don't seem to remember well the ancient Greek family tragedies. We need to make not a family but a civil community of neighbors, who may neither spend nor look alike but share a desire for truthful history—an alert curiosity about the stories and the lives of our neighbors and a respect both for difference—and for privacy. We must get the metaphors right; we are neither brothers nor sisters here in Minnesota, nor even cousins. We are neighbors, all us *ethnics,* and that fact imposes on us a stricter obligation than blood and, to the degree to which we live up to it, makes us civilized.

As both Minnesotans and Americans, none of us can escape the fact that we *ethnics,* in historic terms, have hardly settled here for the length of a sneeze. Most of us have barely had time to lose the language of our ancestors or to produce protein-stuffed children half a foot taller than ourselves. What does a mere century or a little better amount to in history? Even the oldest settlers—the almost ur-inhabitants, the Dakota and Ojibwe—emigrated here from elsewhere on the continent. The Jeffers Petroglyphs in southwest Minnesota are probably the oldest evidence we have of any human habitation. They are still and will most likely remain only shadowy tellers of any historic truth about us. Who made this language? History is silent. The only clear facts scholars agree on about these mysterious pictures carved in hard red Sioux quartzite is that they were the work of neither of the current native tribes and can be scientifically dated only between the melting of the last glacier and the arrival of the first European settlers in the territory. They seem very old to the eye. It is good for us, I think, that our history begins not with certainty, but with mystery, cause for wonder rather than warfare.

In 1978, before the first edition of this ethnic survey appeared, a researcher came to Minneota to interview local people for information about the Icelanders. Tiny though their numbers, the Icelanders were a real ethnic group with their own language, history, and habits of mind. They settled in the late nineteenth century in three small clumps around Minneota. At that time, I could still introduce this researcher to a few old ladies born in Iceland and to a dozen children of immigrants who grew up with English as a second language, thus with thick accents. The old still prayed the Lord's Prayer in Icelandic, to them the language of Jesus himself, and a handful of people could still read the ancient poems and sagas in the leather-covered editions brought as treasures from the old country. But two decades have wiped out that primary source. The first generation is gone, only a few alert and alive in the second, and the third speaks only English—real Americans in hardly a century. What driblets of Icelandic blood remain are mixed with a little of this, a little of that. The old thorny names, so difficult to pronounce, have been respelled, then corrected for sound.

Is this the end of ethnicity? The complete meltdown into history evaporated into global marketing anonymity? I say no. On a late October day, a letter arrives from a housewife in Nevis, Minnesota. She's never met me, but she's been to Iceland now and met unknown cousins she found on an Internet genealogy search. The didactic voice in my books reminds her of her father's voice: "He could've said that. Are we *all* literary?" We've never met, she confesses, but she gives me enough of her family tree to convince me that we might be cousins fifteen generations back. She is descended, she says with pride, from the Icelandic law speaker in 1063, Gunnar the Wise. She knows now that she is not alone in history. She has shadowing names, even dates, in her very cells. She says—with more smug pride—that her vinarterta (an Icelandic immigrant prune cake that is often the last surviving ghost of the old country) is better than any she ate in Iceland. She invites me to sample a piece if I ever get to Nevis. Who says there is no profit and joy in ethnicity? That killjoy has obviously never tasted vinarterta!

I think what is happening in this letter, both psychologically and culturally, happens simultaneously in the lives of hundreds of thousands of Minnesotans and countless millions of Americans. Only the details differ, pilaf, jiaozi, fry bread, collards, latkes, or menudo rather than vinarterta, but the process and the object remain the same. We came to this cold flat place so far from the sea in wave after wave of immigration—filling up the steadily fewer empty places in this vast midsection of a continent—but for all of us, whatever the reason for our arrival: poverty, political upheaval, ambition—we check most of our history, and thus our inner life, at the door of the new world. For a while, old habits and even the language carry on, but by the third generation, history is lost. Yet America's history, much less Minnesota's, is so tiny, so new, so uncertain, so much composed of broken connections—and now of vapid media marketing—that we feel a loneliness for a history that stretches back farther into the life of the planet. We want more cousins so that, in the best sense, we can be better neighbors. We can acquire interior weight that will keep us rooted in our new homes. That is why we need to read these essays on the ethnic history of Minnesota. We need to meet those neighbors and listen to new stories.

We need also the concrete underpinning of facts that they provide to give real body to our tribal myths if those myths are not to drift off into nostalgic vapor. Svenskarnas Dag and Santa Lucia Day will not tell us much about the old Sweden that disgorged so many of its poor to Minnesota. At the height of the Vietnam War, an old schoolmate of mine steeled his courage to confess to his stern Swedish father that he was thinking both of conscientious objection and, if that didn't work, escape to Canada. He expected patriotic disdain, even contempt. Instead the upright old man wept and cried, "So soon again!" He had left Sweden early in the century to avoid the compulsory military draft but told that history to none of his children. The history of our arrival here does not lose its nobility by being filled with draft-dodging, tubercular lungs, head lice, poverty, failure. It gains humanity. We are all members of a very big club—and not an exclusive one.

I grew up in western Minnesota surrounded by accents: Icelandic, Norwegian, Swedish, Belgian, Dutch, German, Polish, French Canadian, Irish, even a Yankee or two, a French Jewish doctor, and a Japanese chicken sexer in Dr. Kerr's chicken hatchery. As a boy, I thought that a fair-sized family of nations. Some of those tribes have declined almost to extinction, and new immigrants have come to replace them: Mexican, Somali, Hmong, and Balkan. Relations are sometimes awkward as the old ethnicities bump their aging dispositions against the new, forgetting that their own grandparents spoke English strangely, dressed in odd clothes, and ate foods that astonished and sometimes repulsed their neighbors. History does not cease moving at the exact moment we begin to occupy it comfortably.

I've taught many Laotian students in my freshman English classes at Southwest State University in Marshall. I always assign papers on family history. For many children of the fourth generation, the real stories have evaporated, but for the Hmong, they are very much alive—escape followed by gunfire, swimming the Mekong, a childhood in Thai refugee camps. One student brought a piece of his mother's intricate embroidery to class and translated its symbolic storytelling language for his classmates. Those native-born children of farmers will now be haunted for life by the dark water of the Mekong. Ethnic history is alive and surprisingly well in Minnesota.

Meanwhile the passion for connection—thus a craving for a deeper history—has blossomed grandly in my generation and the new one in front of it. A Canadian professional genealogist at work at an immigrant genealogical center at Hofsos in north Iceland assures me, as fact, that genealogy has surpassed, in raw numbers, both stamp and coin collecting as a hobby. What will it next overtake? Baseball cards? Rock and roll 45 rpms? It's a sport with a future, and these essays on ethnic history are part of the evidence of its success.

I've even bought a little house in Hofsos, thirty miles south of the Arctic Circle where in the endless summer light I watch loads of immigrant descendants from Canada and the United States arrive clutching old brown-tone photos, yellowed letters in languages they don't read, the misspelled name of Grandpa's farm. They feed their information into computers and comb through heavy books, hoping to find the history lost when their ancestors simplified their names at Ellis Island or in Quebec. To be ethnic, somehow, is to be human. Neither can we escape it, nor should we want to. You cannot interest yourself in the lives of your neighbors if you don't take sufficient interest in your own.

Minnesotans often jokingly describe their ethnic backgrounds as "mongrel"—a little of this, a little of that, who knows what? But what a gift to be a mongrel! So many ethnicities and so little time in life to track them down! You will have to read many of these essays to find out who was up to what, when. We should also note that every one of us on this planet is a mongrel, thank God. The mongrel is the strongest and longest lived of dogs—and of humans, too. Only the dead are pure—and then, only in memory, never in fact. Mongrels do not kill each other to maintain the pure ideology of the tribe. They just go on mating, acquiring a richer ethnic history with every passing generation. So I commend this series to you. Let me introduce you to your neighbors. May you find pleasure and wisdom in their company.

Hmong

IN MINNESOTA

Left to right: Nhia Yang, Peter Yang, May Lee Vang, Youa Vang, and Bo Vang, St. Paul, ca. 1987

HMONG REFUGEES have been settling in Minnesota since the mid-1970s; along the way they have experienced both intense hardship and rewarding success. Many have received much-needed support in their new home at the same time that they have made significant contributions to the state. Yet many Minnesotans and other Americans understand neither the broad involvement of Hmong refugees in recent American history nor the unique circumstances that led them to Minnesota in the first place. Despite efforts to raise awareness, common questions remain: why are there so many Hmong people in the Twin Cities? Why do they choose Minnesota? Why do they not return to their own country? Details about the Hmong in Minnesota—their arrival, adjustment, cultural practices, and successes, gathered through archival research and interviews—will offer a better understanding of one of Minnesota's newest immigrant groups.

A Brief History of the Hmong in Laos

There is no Hmong nation state. People of Hmong ethnicity migrated from southern China to Southeast Asia beginning in the early 1800s. Although today a significant number of Hmong live in Laos, Thailand, and Vietnam, all of those who came to the United States as refugees were from Laos.

America's Covert Operations in Laos

The Hmong people of Laos have a complicated history of ties to the United States as a result of superpower struggles during the Cold War. As an extension of the war in Vietnam, more than 30,000 Hmong men and boys served as America's foot soldiers in Laos from 1961 to 1973.[1]

After earning independence from French colonial rule in 1954, Laos had become a neutral nation: the 1954 Geneva Peace Accords prevented any foreign troops from being stationed there. As the United States sought to prevent the spread of Communism in Asia, however, American government officials circumvented the Geneva Accords restriction by creating a Program Evaluation Office (PEO) in Laos in 1955. The office was staffed by military officers to administer its military aid program; these men wore civilian clothing until 1961. When it became clear that Communist momentum throughout Indochina had increased, the United States gave up any pretense of abiding by the 1954 agreements, choosing instead to augment the number of American military advisors in Laos.[2]

In late 1961, agents of the U.S. Central Intelligence Agency (CIA) contacted and convinced the Hmong military leader, Colonel (later General) Vang Pao of the Royal Lao Army, to work with the Americans. Rather than sending American foot soldiers into Laos, the CIA proposed to train local volunteers into guerrilla fighters. In return, the Hmong, who lived mostly in the northeastern part of the country, would be provided with food, medicine, protection, and military training and supplies. From 1961 until the cease-fire in 1973, the U.S. government provided military aid to the Royal Lao government disguised under the facade of economic expansion and under the auspices of the U.S. Agency for International Development (USAID). The Laos war was overseen by the U.S. ambassador, run by the CIA, and supported by the U.S. military—all without the consent and knowledge of Congress.[3]

The war made a significant impact on Hmong life. Prior to American involvement in Laos, the Hmong were primarily agrarian and few had access to formal education. During the war years, USAID funds were used to build schools in locations with a high concentration of displaced Hmong, making it possible for many young people to attend school

Vang Pao, 2006

Vang Pao: Military Leader

General Vang Pao achieved his military status through service in the Royal Lao Army. As a teenager, he fought the Japanese in World War II; in the 1950s, he served under the French in their disastrous war against the Vietnamese nationalists. When the CIA was looking for someone to lead a covert operation in Laos during the early 1960s, Vang Pao seemed the obvious choice. By the mid-1960s, he was in charge of the Military Two region of northeastern Laos, where the majority of Hmong people resided. The general led the Hmong people and other ethnic groups to fight alongside American military advisers in northern Laos for nearly fifteen years. His tenacity and his alliance with the Americans jeopardized the new Lao government. Consequently, in mid-May 1975, he and some of his military leaders along with their family members and select civilians were airlifted out of Laos. General Vang Pao has resided in Montana and California but frequently visits various Hmong communities throughout the United States. While there are many new and emerging leaders in the Hmong American community, General Vang Pao continues to symbolize a historic, transformative period in Hmong history.

for the first time. Yia Lee remembers, "[It was] only when Vang Pao built all these schools that more had the opportunity. When we went to school, the first couple of rows were girls and the rest of the seven or eight [rows] were boys. But girls usually didn't go far in school because of other responsibilities. In the higher levels, you rarely saw girls." May A Yang, who had been fortunate enough to attend school in the mid-1950s, was one of the few female teachers. She remembers, "In 1964, we lived in Long Cheng. They asked for volunteers who were literate to help teach others. So, as one of [the] few women who were literate, I became a teacher. I taught until 1972. My husband, Vang Xue, who was a pilot, died in the line of duty on October 18, 1972. After that, I didn't teach anymore. After he died, I started to sew women's clothes and was essentially a businesswoman."[4]

USAID also built a hospital in Sam Thong. As the number of wounded soldiers and casualties increased, so did the need for hospital staff. Many young women were recruited to attend nurse training. Choua Thao was the first Hmong "nurse." She worked with Diana Dick, an International Voluntary Services (IVS) staff member and nurse, to develop training curriculum. However, Choua was solely responsible for recruitment and training. She recalls

> Around 1965, I was working with Pop [Edgar Buell]. I was in the airplane going around to recruit nurse trainees. I was so young, just twenty-one. I had four children. I taught the nurse classes. I flew in helicopters and other airplanes from one village to another to recruit. Pop told me that I was in charge. Altogether, I had one hundred nurses, all single girls. Each cohort was about thirty students. Some girls started but never finished. The majority were Hmong, but there were Khamu, Mien, Lao, and other ethnic groups. . . . They lived in dorms. The expectations were that they learned. They had people to cook and clean for them, but it was expected that they go to work whenever needed. Some of them, I had to teach them ABCs so that they could read the labels on prescriptions. After the training, they stayed and worked at the hospital, at Sam Thong and Naxu. I was the administrator and instructor.

Diana, who was known as Nurse Dee, reminisced about her work with Choua: "I never knew how [Choua] was able to recruit the girls. We worked very hard, but because I didn't speak their language, it was Choua who made everything happen." The Sam Thong hospital was taken over by Communist forces in 1971, resulting in the flight and resettlement of thousands of displaced persons to CIA headquarters at Long Cheng.[5]

Meanwhile, the American public and most members of Congress were not aware of the CIA's clandestine army. Journalists were not allowed on the Long Cheng premises. The years of training, ground and air operations, radio networks, and supplied weaponry remained highly classified throughout most of the Vietnam War. The distance between the CIA base and urban centers meant that other Lao people were not aware of these activities, either. Gaoly Yang describes her experience of going to school in the capitol city of Vientiane and visiting Long Cheng:

Now you know that it was a secret war. People didn't know about it then. Regular people didn't know. Just like every day now you have refugees here, but your average Minnesotan does not know much about them. The Lao people who were knowledgeable were the people involved with the Americans. But it was two totally different worlds. When I come to Long Cheng, I see my people. When you go back to Vientiane, you don't know that there is any war going on. That's how drastic the situation was. When you're in Long Cheng, you hear missile attacks and gunshots in the distance, but that was just a part of life. When you're in Vientiane, it's

Women and War

The work of nurses from Hmong and other ethnic groups supported the clandestine war. Many parents initially considered nursing to be dirty work, but the status nurses enjoyed changed greatly as they received monthly salaries, which many used to support their parents. The training these young women received was hands-on, their responsibilities ranging from prescription distribution to operation assistants. The intensity of the work proved too challenging for some.

Left to right: Song Chow, Diana Dick, and Choua Thao, ca. 1966 at Sam Thong hospital

totally different. Unless you're in both worlds, you wouldn't even begin to understand.[6]

As the war years progressed, the role of guerrilla fighters changed from primarily collecting intelligence information and engaging in smaller "attack and retreat" battles with Communist forces in the early 1960s to tasks such as rescuing downed American pilots and participating in larger-scale battles by the second half of that decade.

Following the peace treaty in January 1973, representatives of the different Lao factions worked to create a coalition government. As in Vietnam, it soon became clear that the left's influence was gaining momentum and those who had allied with foreigners and had a higher military rank would be viewed as a threat to the new regime. Fear ran rampant as people began to see friends, relatives, and neighbors taken away to "seminar camps" from which many did not return. By early May 1975, the Hmong at Long Cheng knew they would not be able to hold out there much longer. On the advice of CIA case officer Jerry Daniels, an air evacuation of General Vang Pao, high-ranking officers, and their families began on May 11. When word of the evacuation spread, thousands fought their way inside the planes: many civilians were airlifted while some military personnel missed the flights. When the last plane departed on May 14, those left behind scurried to find their own way out.[7]

Association with the Americans brought some benefits to the Hmong; however, the lengthy war led to the displacement of thousands of Hmong, many of whom could not return to their former way of life. Out of an approximate population of 350,000 before the war, an estimated 17,000 soldiers were killed and uncounted numbers were wounded and as many as 50,000 civilians were killed or wounded. These estimates do not take into account the thousands who died while trying to escape from Laos from 1975 through the 1990s.[8]

Escape Narratives

The air evacuation effort brought about 2,500 Hmong out of Long Cheng to a military base in Ban Namphong, Thailand. Uncertain about how their involvement with the Americans would affect their future in Laos, thousands more escaped to Thailand, where they remained in refugee camps set up by the United Nations High Commissioner for Refugees. Major Shoua Vang reflected on the airlift:

> That day, my wife [and] younger brother went in the C-130. My older brother, Chong Koua, rode in the plane with Colonel Vang Kao. At that moment, I had no idea if I would return. I had over three hundred slides/pictures. I was afraid that if the Vietnamese caught me with them, I would easily be killed. I regret it tremendously. . . . I had no idea about the future. When our plane ascended, you could hear gunshots. All you could do was wait to see if the plane would be hit by any bullets. A thought did cross my mind at that moment that perhaps this may be the last time I'd see Long Cheng.[9]

The vast majority of those who escaped were not fortunate enough to be airlifted. Those who traveled on foot from May 1975 throughout the early 1990s met much hardship and tragedy. While some successfully crossed the Mekong River, the border between Laos and Thailand, others became fatally ill, drowned, or were captured by soldiers of the new regime. Four former refugees remember their escapes:

Toua Thao:

> The reason I left was that I heard from some Lao friends *aib noob* [communist soldiers] were looking for me and they wanted to talk to me. I had heard rumors that others had been arrested and sent to seminar camps. I hadn't seen it myself, but I heard that if arrested, you could be jailed or killed. . . . I was a field assistant for USAID. So, I decided to leave. . . . We crossed the river by boat at night. In the camps, we only considered coming to the U.S.

Mao Vang Lee:

> We planned our escape with other members of our family. We had to pretend as though we were just going to the city for work. My husband and I had been entrusted with several of our relatives' teenagers. We had to cross at nighttime so that the border patrols wouldn't see us. . . . We did finally make it to Thailand. There was no doubt in our minds that we would come to the U.S.

Shong Yang:

> We swam across the river. Most of us knew how to swim. For others, we cut bamboos to build small rafts. Once we reached Nong Khai camp, I fell ill and had to stay at the hospital for eighteen days. When I returned to the camp, I didn't know what to do. I was a young person and had no credentials to come to the U.S. My older brother had died during a feud right after we crossed the river. My brother's father-in-law died while crossing the river. Only his wife and two daughters made it. So, when we applied, we decided to say that I was her son and that her husband was a soldier who had died while crossing.

Tong Vang:

> I was all by myself. I had my clothes on my body,
> wore flip-flops, and carried a small sack. . . . Once
> on the boat, the guide told me to lay down. He
> rushed me straight across to the other side. He
> let me out and returned to the Lao side. The per-
> son who met me on the Thai side told me to pay
> him. I told him I had already paid the other guy.
> He then asked me to give him a little [to] buy
> cigarettes. . . . Once I reached the road, there was
> no one in sight. I saw two houses on the other
> side. I was going to go ask them where Xixangmai
> [was,] where the others were staying. A van came
> by. . . . At that time, a Lao man sitting inside said
> to me that it was okay to get in. They were patrols
> that General [Vang Pao] and the Americans had
> asked to pick up the Hmong who crossed over to
> Thailand. So, I got in the van and, fortunately, I
> was taken straight to the camp.

These escape narratives reflect the experiences of the more
than 100,000 Hmong refugees who were admitted to
the United States during the last quarter of the twentieth
century.[10]

Refugee Resettlement in the United States

Resettlement is one strategy for coping with refugees;
other, often less desirable, alternatives are repatriation or
extended time in refugee camps or in countries unwilling
to offer permanent residence or protection. Hmong who
left Laos due to persecution became political refugees and
thus were eligible for relief and protection under international law. At the international level, resettlement involves
the transfer of selected refugees from a nation in which

they have sought protection to a third country which has agreed to admit them and to offer permanent resident status. Such status provides a resettled refugee and his or her family or dependents with access to civil, political, economic, social, and cultural rights similar to those enjoyed by citizens. The status also carries with it the opportunity to eventually become a naturalized citizen of the resettlement country.[11]

Policies and Programs

When the U.S. Congress passed the Indochina Migration and Refugee Assistance Act in May 1975, it included only refugees from Vietnam and Cambodia. After much advocacy by American supporters and Hmong community leaders, the act was extended in June 1976 to include refu-

---

Hmong Migration to Minnesota, 1976–2004

1976   Indochina Migration and Refugee Assistance Act (1975) extended to Laotians, including ethnic Lao, Hmong, and other minority groups involved with Americans during the Vietnam War. Arrival of the first Hmong refugees in Minnesota through the refugee resettlement program.

1977   Indochinese Refugee Resettlement Office transferred from the Minnesota governor's office to the state's Public Welfare Department.

1980   U.S. Refugee Act establishes education and training for refugees prior to departure for the United States. At federal level, the Office of Refugee Resettlement (ORR) created within the U.S. Department of Health and Human Services. In Minnesota, the state Health Advisory Committee on Indochinese Refugees formed as ad hoc committee of Minnesota Medical Association to address health-related issues.

1981   Minnesota's Refugee Program Office established, operating under two governing bodies: the Indochinese Advisory Council and the Minnesota State Refugee Advisory Council.

1992   United Nations–sponsored Ban Vinai refugee camp in Thailand closed: Hmong refugees awaiting resettlement to the United States moved to Phanat Nikhom; those opting to return to Laos moved to Ban Napho and Chiang Kham.[1]

1995   Chiang Kham camp closed, halting resettlement of all Hmong refugees.

2003   U.S. State Department announces it will resettle up to 15,000 Hmong refugees living in Wat Tham Krabok.

2004   St. Paul mayor Randy Kelly leads delegation to assess health conditions of Wat Tham Krabok refugees in early 2004; the first families arrive in Minnesota that summer.

---

gees from Laos. Several western countries agreed to accept Hmong refugees. The vast majority, about 130,000 people, came to the United States, while about 10,000 immigrated to France and a couple thousand chose Canada and Australia. In the United States, California, Minnesota, and Wisconsin have had the largest Hmong American populations during the last thirty years.[12]

Since World War II, admission of refugees into the United States has been on an ad hoc basis, with Congress responding independently to each political crisis. Not until the Refugee Act of 1980 were policies and procedures for refugee resettlement set in place. The act established the Office of Refugee Resettlement within the U.S. Department of Health and Human Services to work with state and local agencies. The U.S. resettlement program is designed to function as a public-private partnership, with nongovernmental organizations participating in every step of the process. The national voluntary agency system works with local private agencies through which groups, congregations, and individuals agree to be sponsors and to provide initial food, clothing, housing, and employment to the refugees. The primary agencies involved in resettlement of the Hmong were U.S. Catholic Conference (USCC), Lutheran Immigration and Refugee Services (LIRS), and Church World Services, all of which operated in many other locations throughout the country. The International Institute of Minnesota represented the American Council for Nationality; Catholic Charities of the St. Paul, Winona, and St. Cloud dioceses worked directly with USCC; and Lutheran Social Services of Minnesota was the local resettlement arm of LIRS. Staff members of these agencies served as liaisons to camp resettlement personnel.[13]

Minnesota's climate does not recommend the state as a logical new home for the Hmong. While agencies in states such as California resettled the largest number, Minnesota's strong faith-based, voluntary community was instrumental in the initial resettlement of Hmong refugees. In the mid- to late 1970s, families in refugee camps could not be resettled until an American sponsor was identified. After 1980, chain migration or family reunification from refugee camps and secondary migration from other states contributed to the growth of the Hmong population in the state.

The First Arrivals

When the first agency-resettled Hmong refugees arrived at the Minneapolis–St. Paul International Airport in 1976, they faced more than culture shock. Everything they encountered was unfamiliar: climate, language, clothes, smells, food, and customs. Most were exhausted and bewildered after months of living in crowded refugee camps and days of international travel. Some arrived with family members at their side; others had no idea where their closest relatives had been taken or if they would ever see them again. After having barely eaten for days, when faced with the language barrier and the strangeness of American cuisine, some were too perplexed to eat. Many walked out of the airport in sandals and t-shirts, only to be confronted by the brute force of a snowy Minnesota winter. Everything was suddenly different.

Reflecting on the plane ride from Thailand to the United States, Ly Vang recalls much anxiety. She and her husband had come on the same flight with other Hmong families; to some extent, they did not begin to feel alone until they landed in Chicago, where everyone went their separate ways. She explains

> It was at this moment of separation that you began to feel lost. You wonder about where you're going, what you'll do, and what kind of life you will have. How will we survive? Will we be safe? You think back to all the events of the war, and you wonder if

you would experience the same things. How are we going to sleep? What kind of house will we live in? What kind of food will we eat? We did know that we were going to America and that we had a sponsor. But we didn't know that our sponsors would greet us at the airport. We imagined that an immigration officer would pick us up and drop us off somewhere.[14]

Depending on the sponsors' preparation, refugee families received varied support. Despite feeling isolated, May Ia Lee remembers appreciating her sponsor's efforts:

We arrived in winter. The sponsors brought us winter coats. Our sponsors had an apartment ready for us. They also made sure there was food ready for us. We lived in [Liberty] Plaza[, St. Paul]. Our sponsor helped us, but there were others in her church that helped, too. The first few days were so odd. I don't know about others, but for us, our sponsors had well prepared our home for us. Pots and pans, blankets, pillows, sofas—everything. They were wonderful to us. Materially, we had everything, but our hearts were empty. I didn't know any English. Once you go outside of the house and to the public, you become someone mute. You felt so little because you didn't know anything.[15]

Most Americans knew very little about Southeast Asian ethnic groups. Moreover, Minnesotans generally had never heard of the Hmong prior to the arrival of this ethnic group in the state. Kathleen Vallenga became interested in sponsoring refugees after seeing the Vietnamese "boat people" struggling on television while she was hospitalized in 1975. Just as she had needed help from others, she was inspired to offer assistance when she could. Her leadership brought

Leng Vang and May Ia Lee and their family to St. Paul in February 1976. Vallenga recalls how the refugees educated their sponsors about the various ethnic groups:

> Our church, Dayton Presbyterian, was so small. When I convinced them that we should sponsor refugees, we thought it would be Vietnamese. That's who we saw on TV. We've never heard of Hmong. So I went to Macalester Plymouth and asked them to partner with us. We had a committee meeting. We had a plan where we would provide free housing for the first year for the refugees at Liberty Plaza. When Olga Zoltai from the International Institute called us, she said we would sponsor a family from Laos. So I said, okay, Laotians. But, when we got the slip, it said *Meo,* which we learned later . . . was a derogatory Laotian term. We still didn't know the name Hmong. It wasn't until the family arrived that we learned about Hmong. They said, "Hmong," and we said, "What's that?" Leng explained. He had enough soldier English that he could communicate. So that's how it happened that we had Hmong. The International Institute also knew nothing about Hmong.[16]

While some families lived with their sponsors, many others were provided housing support. Limited financial resources meant few housing options. Like other immigrant groups, Hmong refugees were concentrated in poor, urban neighborhoods, including Phillips and Near North in Minneapolis and Frogtown in St. Paul. In addition to high populations in particular neighborhoods, from the late 1970s throughout the 1990s Hmong refugees dominated the public housing complexes that were previously occupied primarily by African Americans, Latinos, and low-income whites.

May Ia Lee with her mother and children in front of their apartment in the early 1980s

A New Home: Liberty Plaza

Although Hmong refugees became residents in all public housing complexes throughout the Twin Cities, the largest group initially was at Liberty Plaza, located on the southwest corner of Interstate 94 and Western Avenue. Sponsored and managed by Dayton Presbyterian Church in St. Paul, Liberty Plaza offered affordable housing for low-income community members. Because the first family to be sponsored through the International Institute of Minnesota was cosponsored by Dayton Presbyterian, they were provided housing at Liberty Plaza. Then, as other friends and relatives arrived, residents recruited them to live there. Liberty Plaza became a lively place where Hmong children could together while their parents and grandparents attended English classes at the community center and where Hmong refugees could congregate and celebrate their traditions.

Mani Vang Heu (second from left) and friends dressed in Hmong clothes outside Liberty Plaza, ca. mid-1980s

Beyond financial necessity, the Hmong clustered together as a means of survival. The first public housing location the Hmong called home was Liberty Plaza, but other complexes in St. Paul with significant numbers of Hmong residents included the Mount Airy, McDonough, and Roosevelt homes. Across the river, the largest concentration was in the Sumner Field Housing Project and, in the early resettlement years, in particular apartment buildings in south Minneapolis. Facing rental challenges because of large family sizes but also gradually achieving financial independence, the Hmong community eventually saw home-ownership increase exponentially. By 2000, 54 percent of the Hmong population in Minnesota owned their homes.[17]

Secondary Migration

The initial wave of Hmong refugees dispersed throughout various parts of the United States. Still, some of the first families eventually connected and found ways to regroup in the Twin Cities metropolitan area, both through their own contacts and with the help of their sponsors. This chain migration occurred on multiple levels.

Many second-wave refugees share a home with numerous residents because Hmong families traditionally have many children and their households are often multigenerational. This two-parent household also includes a grandmother.

Mao Vang Lee:

> I arrived in Manchester, Connecticut, on August 16,
> 1978. It is a town with very few minorities. We were
> one of only a few Hmong families. We went to work
> right away. Although it was hard at first, we man-
> aged to stay and build a small Hmong community
> in Connecticut. We have three sons. When we first
> came to Minnesota many years ago during the New
> Year celebration and soccer festivals, my children
> said, "Mom and dad: we belong here. People here
> look like us. We don't belong in Connecticut." So, in
> 1995, we moved to Minnesota.

Tong Vang:

> I decided to come to Minnesota because my cousin
> had already been sponsored by a family in this state.

Mai Yer Lee:

> My mother-in-law and my brother-in-law had
> moved to Minnesota. They moved here because my
> older sister and her husband moved to follow their
> relatives in Iowa. Then, on to Minnesota. They sent
> us cassettes to tell us how nice things were here.

Gaoly Yang:

> For those of us who first arrived here, we felt that
> this was a friendlier environment for newcomers
> based on the fact that we were given the opportuni-
> ties to work. I recruited my sister, who [had] reset-
> tled in Philadelphia. My husband encouraged many
> of his relatives to move here. After learning about
> our lives here in St. Paul, they want to settle here. So
> it is the Hmong people who helped and recruited
> each other to create their own community here.

Americans have initiated a few [recruitments], but, truly, they wouldn't have encouraged people to come here at a high rate.[18]

Like other immigrant and refugee groups, the Hmong seek to be with those who share their culture and language. Building community also allows refugees to provide mutual support beyond what is offered by sponsors and service organizations. Because Hmong society is organized around the family and its extended kinship network, not around the individual or the nuclear family, this congregating is crucial to successful resettlement. The State Department and early sponsors did not understand this cultural preference; as a result, many first-wave Hmong refugees

---

Who Was First?

Which Hmong family was the first to arrive in Minnesota? Who was the first Hmong child born in the state? These frequently asked questions can be difficult to answer, in part because of sparse documentation in the early years of resettlement.

Several individuals have made conflicting claims of being the first Hmong to arrive in Minnesota. In interviews, many community members refer to Leng Wong (formerly Vang) and May Ia Lee's family as the first to be resettled in Minnesota: they arrived here on February 16, 1976. Kathleen Vallenga reported that she was unaware of any other families being sponsored before Leng and May Ia's arrival. However, she was not certain they were the first family. As it turns out, they were not.[2]

Dang Her and his wife, Shoua Moua, came to Minnesota on November 5, 1975, making them officially the first Hmong family to arrive in the state. However, their journey to Minnesota was not through the formal refugee resettlement process. Dang, a onetime field assistant for the U.S. Agency for International Development, became close to a USAID staff member, a Minnesotan who, in collaboration with his congregation, sponsored Dang and Shoua after learning they were displaced in Thailand.[3]

Bill Her, 1976

---

felt isolated and helpless. By the early 1980s, the American Council for Nationality had identified St. Paul as one of several "impacted" areas—sites with high numbers of refugees relative to available jobs, housing, and services—and the State Department implemented a "planned placement" effort to resettle refugees in locations throughout the United States. This policy successfully distributed the refugees, but soon Hmong people moved closer to each other and built larger communities together.[19]

Hmong Minnesotans Today

A common perception is that all people of Hmong ethnicity are refugees regardless of how long they have lived in

Dang Her with his sons in the 1990s. Bill is in the back row, fourth from the left.

May A Yang and son, Paul Vang, 1976

Similar to the confusion about which family arrived first is the uncertainty regarding the first Hmong child born in Minnesota. Interviews with these first families confirmed that Bill Her, the son of Dang Her and Shoua Moua, was the first baby born to a resettled family. Bill arrived on February 5, 1976. His family initially lived in Anoka but later moved to St. Paul to be part of the growing Hmong community. The second child to be born to Hmong refugee parents was Kao Lee Thao, whose birthday is May 21, 1976. Although her parents, Mao Heu Thao and Toua Thao, lived in La Crescent, Minnesota, Kao Lee was born in La Crosse, Wisconsin. The third child, Paul Vang, was born in St. Paul on October 15, 1976, to May A Yang and Tong Vang.

this country. Migration patterns have been diverse from early on: in addition to direct resettlement from refugee camps to Minnesota, U.S. immigration laws permitting family reunification have allowed many Hmong who did not leave Laos or who initially resettled in other countries to immigrate to the United States. The Hmong American population ranges from children born to refugee parents to those with visitor visas from other countries of resettlement to spouses of Hmong Americans from Laos and Thailand. Today's Hmong Minnesotans likely fit into one of the following categories:

· Those who arrived in Minnesota as refugees and have remained in the state;
· Children who are U.S.–born;
· Those who initially resettled in other parts of the country and have migrated here;
· Those who initially resettled in other nations and who immigrated to the United States through family reunification opportunities and now are legal residents;
· Those who initially resettled in other nations and who came to the United States with visitor visas and have either adjusted their immigration status or are overstaying their visas;
· Those who never left Laos and are sponsored by Hmong U.S. citizens through family reunification policies;
· Women and a few men from Laos who are brought to the United States as spouses of Hmong U.S. citizens; or
· Women from other countries of resettlement brought to the United States as brides of Hmong U.S. citizens.[20]

Migrant Stories

In 1974, when Bauz L. Nengchu was a sophomore at Dara Samouth high school in Laos, she received a letter from her parents, who urged her to leave the country at once and join them in France, where they had been living since 1972. Less than a year later, Laos fell to Communist forces, inspiring a mass exodus of Hmong refugees to Thailand. Should Bauz have waited a little longer, she would have shared this harsh experience with them. In 1979, while visiting relatives living in the United States, Bauz met her future husband, Vang Cheng. They married the following year and have lived in Minnesota since 1986. Bauz has two sons and three daughters.[4]

Left to right: Lysao Lyfoung (father), Jimvang Nengchu (son), Bauz L. Nengchu, and Maysai V. Lyfoung (mother), 2006

Yee Her immigrated to the United States in 1988. In early 2001, he visited relatives in Laos, where he met Lyda Vang. Lyda's parents had stayed in Laos, where her father was a pharmacist and her mother an eye doctor. Lyda had earned a college degree there. When Yee asked her to marry him, she and her parents agreed that it would be the best situation for her. Yee processed the appropriate immigration application, and Lyda joined him in Minnesota in December 2001. They and their daughter live in Brooklyn Center.

Yee Her and Lyda Vang with daughter Alincy Her

Adjusting to Modern Life

The resettling of refugees in Minnesota from such a starkly different culture was never simple. Most Hmong came from agrarian backgrounds and were unfamiliar with both

Minnesota Counties with Hmong Residents
Hmong Americans were present in forty of Minnesota's eighty-seven counties by 2000.

Counting Hmong Minnesotans

The 2000 census counted 186,310 Hmong Americans in the United States, of which 41,800 resided in Minnesota, up from 17,764 in 1990—a growth surge of 135 percent in a single decade. Community leaders and service organizations dispute these numbers, however, estimating a significantly higher population of as many as 70,000 Hmong Minnesotans in 2000. Two tables show the geographic distribution of Hmong Americans throughout the state.[5]

Metropolitan-Area Cities with Hmong Populations

CITY	TOTAL
St. Paul	24,389
Minneapolis	9,595
Brooklyn Center	1,346
Brooklyn Park	1,226
Maplewood	685
Woodbury	264
Blaine	185
Roseville	117
Eagan	104
Burnsville	72
Bloomington	55
Maple Grove	40
Apple Valley	34
Savage	29
Richfield	19
St. Louis Park	9
Plymouth	8
Minnetonka	7
Hopkins	6
Eden Prairie	4
Edina	2
Total	38,196

Non–Metropolitan-Area Cities with Hmong Populations

CITY	TOTAL
Rochester	211
Winona	199
Tracy	169
Duluth	147
St. Cloud	57
Faribault	42
Mankato	37
Marshall	36
Austin	2
Worthington	1
Total	901

twentieth-century technology and the complexities of urban life. Few lived in Laotian cities prior to the "secret war" years. Hmong society had been largely influenced by life in the mountains, slash-and-burn agriculture, the practice of animism and ancestral worship, and a patriarchal family and clan system. Isolation in the mountainous regions of northern Laos allowed them some freedom in running their own affairs; it also held many in poverty and prevented them from pursuing educational and economic opportunities that others enjoyed.[21]

When May A Yang arrived in Minnesota in 1976, she was amazed at the variety of items available at grocery stores. She recalls, "Our sponsor would take us shopping for food. With all of the food choices at the grocery store, it was confusing. It was also funny. There were so many choices. I didn't know who was supposed to pay." Many refugee families experienced this confusion; they also feared various household appliances that were unfamiliar to them.[22]

Refugees, sponsors, and policy makers continually struggled with various assimilation issues. From the beginning, many policy makers were concerned about Hmong refugees adjusting to modern life in America. During the early to mid-1980s, the state implemented several efforts to encourage and support Hmong agricultural practices. The *Hmong Resettlement Study,* conducted by the Office of Refugee Resettlement, lists three categories of farming initiatives created to assist refugees in the United States: community gardening for consumption, community gardening for consumption and commercial sales at a rate that provides supplemental income for participating families, and farming at a commercial rate that provides primary income for participating families.[23]

Of several efforts aimed at preparing Hmong refugees to participate in agricultural activities, two were perhaps most significant: the Minnesota Agricultural Enterprise for New Americans (MAENA) and the Hiawatha Valley Farm Cooperative (HVFC). Launched by the University of Minnesota Agricultural Extension Service in collaboration with Lao Family Community, MAENA was both a training project and business enterprise with the goal of moving families from welfare to self-sufficiency. Coordinator Xang Vang explains how the project got its start: "I took some

Refugee women attending class, early 1980s. One of the first activities refugees engage in is learning English. The federal government provided some funding for language classes, and local resettlement agencies relied heavily on volunteers from churches and colleges and universities to teach English as a Second Language (ESL) classes, which were much in demand.

Hmong farmers to the farmers' market. The director and board members said they didn't want any Hmong farmers because Hmong didn't have any knowledge about vegetables. They felt that if Hmong people sold unsafe vegetables and people became sick, it would be a liability to the Minnesota Grown association. I asked the board if they would be willing to accept us if we received proper training. The board said that if we attended training, then they would allow us to join."[24]

The project initially created the Hmong Farming Cooperative. It began in Oakdale but soon moved to Farmington, where more land was available. The majority of the fifty individuals who completed the eighteen-month training were Hmong. But the project, reliant on grants from private foundations, did not manage to sustain itself and eventually dissolved. However, the training farmers received led many to rent their own small plot of land and grow produce to be sold at the Minneapolis and St. Paul farmers' markets.

The HVFC was coordinated by Church World Services, which also provided technical assistance to participants. HVFC's initial goal was to create a Hmong community consisting of thirty to forty families residing on a 1,300-acre farm in Homer, Minnesota. Families were allotted five acres of land from which they would produce for the co-op and, eventually, earn their primary income. A management council made up of outside volunteers provided assistance and access to markets. For the ten families initially enrolled in the program, classroom and hands-on training in record keeping, management, accounting, and marketing were provided through Hennepin Technical Institute. Former coordinator Tong Vang remembers some of the activities at the farm: "I wanted to make sure that we received proper training. In addition to the swine operation, we also planted cucumbers and other vegetables. The training we received increased our knowledge about operating a farm in this country, and it taught us preventative measures to take when using fertilizer. In the summer, there were days when the families would pick thousands of pounds of pickles. It was an incredible sight."[25]

As their skills increased, the farmers became part of the decision-making process and were introduced to techniques to sustain the project. Some families relocated to Homer. But when local residents protested against the large influx of Hmong families, the program was scaled down, limiting production potential. Shoua Vang, the HVFC bookkeeper, recalls, "When we started, the neighbors were against it, and eventually the funding wasn't there. It wasn't because we failed. It was because the funding support was cut. The people in charge who were responsible for finding money didn't do as they had promised." The project's reliance on grants for staffing and its developers' inability to obtain financing led to its demise in 1985.[26]

HVFC participants took great pride in the swine operation at Homer. The farmers learned how to quickly feed and prepare the hogs to be sold.

Children, men, and women on the Homer farm worked all day long to pick thousands of cucumbers. The cucumbers were processed through a machine that separated them by size: the smaller the cucumber, the higher the price per bushel.

Farmers picking green beans. The farmers sold most of what they grew but saved some for personal consumption, savoring the fresh produce as they did in their homeland.

Beyond these formal programs, the desire to escape city life and all its complexities led small groups of families to relocate to such places as Duluth, Marshall, Rochester, St. Cloud, Tracy, and Worthington. Isolation, language barriers, racism, and lack of a support network made the going difficult for these families. Finding it challenging to thrive in those rural and small-town communities, most returned to the Twin Cities metropolitan area.

Although rural resettlement has been less successful, today more Hmong are moving to suburbs throughout the Twin Cities. By 2000, the west metro cities of Brooklyn Center and Brooklyn Park had gained significant numbers of Hmong Americans; in the east metro, Oakdale, Woodbury, and North St. Paul have also seen increases. University campuses outside of the Twin Cities such as Mankato

State, St. Cloud State, and the University of Minnesota–
Morris have sizeable Hmong American enrollments, but
the students' families do not reside there permanently. Although rural Minnesota communities offer the peace and
tranquility many Hmong families desire, the vast majority
of Minnesota's Hmong American community has settled
in the Twin Cities metropolitan area, where members find
a support network that will help them rebuild their lives in
America.

One American family lived on the Homer farm with the Hmong farmers and their families. The Hmong
farmers worked diligently with their American trainers, but both groups learned from each other: the
trainers observed Hmong farming practices, and the women exchanged recipes and taught each the
other's language. HVFC participants, including Tong Vang (farthest right) and Shoua Vang (front, second
from left), 1984

Those interested in farming have resorted to small gar-
den plots for personal consumption or have signed on as
seasonal workers for American farmers. Some have become more deeply involved by renting land from nearby
farmers and participating in the St. Paul and Minneapolis
farmers' markets.[27]

Marching down the aisles of the Minneapolis and St. Paul farmers' markets, one sees many new vegetables—such as bitter melon, Chinese broccoli, and pumpkin vines—that were not sold here before the mid-1980s. Hmong arts and crafts, in particular *paaj ntaub,* also are regularly available for sale at these locations. *Paaj ntaub* (spelled *paj ntaub* in white Hmong and frequently referred to as *pa ndau* in English) is Hmong textile art that includes cross-stitch embroidery, surface embroidery, and reverse appliqué. Moua Thao and Zoua Yang at the Minneapolis Farmers' Market, 2007

Building Community

Immediately following their arrival in Minnesota, Hmong refugees worked together to rebuild their lives in this new place. Relying on existing Hmong cultural structures, they forged alliances within the Hmong and Lao communities and also pursued opportunities offered by the larger Minnesota community to obtain resources for refugee families and to ease the resettlement process. Although the strategies have evolved over time, they continue to be implemented in various ways.

Clan and Kinship System

Hmong culture and traditions rely on a strong clan and kinship system. Members within a clan lineage trace their ancestors to a common person or share a common tradition of ancestral worship and other rituals, making clan structure and the resulting affiliation a core value in Hmong society. Leadership is determined by age, social and economic status, and gender. Elders are respected for their wisdom and knowledge. In this patriarchal society, men have traditionally been valued over women. The family is under the authority of the male head of household: the oldest male in the family or the oldest adult married son. Like other Asian cultures, the Hmong place greater emphasis on the family and community than on the individual.[28]

Migration initially disrupted this clan system, as family and clan members were torn apart and Hmong refugees sought new ways of community building. In America, new leaders—literate people who spoke English—emerged to serve as intermediaries between the refugee population and mainstream systems and institutions. With respect to traditions and religious rituals, the clan and kinship system has remained intact. However, these new leaders no longer are the eldest community members, many of whom do not possess the English language skills necessary to negotiate both cultures. Self-help organizations, based on the American model of community-based assistance, have emerged as a new community-building and leadership structure for Hmong Americans.

Mutual Assistance Associations

Although Hmong refugees arrived in Minnesota with backgrounds and experiences distinctly different from those of their new neighbors, they shared with them the universal need for community ties. As with many immigrant groups, mutual assistance agencies have played an integral role in community-building efforts for the Hmong in Minnesota. Like other refugee and immigrant self-help groups, many of these agencies began as informal gatherings for social, cultural, and spiritual purposes and offer newcomers opportunities to celebrate their traditions, practice their religion, and find comfort in a common language and culture.[29]

The first few Hmong refugee families to arrive in Minnesota were spread out in a number of locations and received varied support from their sponsors, some of whom tried but failed to fully appreciate the complex issues the newcomers faced. Lacking their customary support network, these families sought to create a sense of community. On July 16, 1977, Hmong living in the Twin Cities area held a meeting to discuss their common problems and to form a self-help association. Resettlement programs designed to aid Indo-Chinese refugees were not meeting the needs of the Hmong; consequently, the Association of Hmong in Minnesota (AHM) was incorporated as a nonprofit organization in September 1977. AHM's objectives were to encourage mutual assistance among the Hmong, to establish communication networks, to advise Americans and Hmong ethnics on each other's culture and history, and to develop elementary educational materials for the Hmong.[30]

Key individuals involved in AHM's development included Tou Fu Vang, Leng Vang, Dang Her, Ya Yang, and Tong Vang. Dang Her recalled the group's early history: "We didn't have any experience with management of an organization. Tou Fu Vang had come to the U.S. as a student, so he spoke English. He had come to Montana with General Vang Pao. He came to Minnesota and helped us to form the Hmong Association. He told us that forming an organization was the only way we could help other refugees that were arriving. I think Leng Vang was the first board chair, then Ya Yang, and then on to Ly Teng." AHM volunteers worked "closely with refugee sponsoring agencies, in-

Lao Family board of directors, ca. 1982. Back row, left to right: Sai Lee, Lao Bao Chang, Yang Xiong, Executive Director Xang Vang, Fue Yang, Houa Moua, Xi Thao. Front row, left to right: Phay Vang, Amphone, Teng Ly, Dang Her, Choua Thao. The first woman to serve on the Lao Family's board of directors was Choua Thao, who in the early 1980s was one of the few Hmong women to be literate in English. Many other women participated in planning meetings and activities, but they did not play an official role. The Lao Family's board of directors is selected by election from the organization's members; for this reason, women continue to play a less significant leadership role.

dividual sponsors, local and state government, the schools, human service providers, and other segments of society in promoting the welfare of Hmong refugees and in facilitating greater cultural understanding between the Hmong people and their American friends." Programs and services included interpretation and translation, assisted job searches, and cultural orientation. The organization's leadership remained almost all male through the mid-1980s.[31]

On June 28, 1980, AHM membership voted to affiliate with Lao Family Community, Inc., a private, nonprofit organization founded by a group of Laotian refugees—including General Vang Pao—in Santa Ana, California,

The Lao Family's community center on University Avenue, St. Paul, houses the Lao Family's offices and offers meeting space for Hmong and non-Hmong community members. On weekends it is frequently rented for weddings, graduation parties, and other gatherings.

in March 1977. By joining this group, the Hmong immigrant generation made explicit the connection to its Lao identity; however, the organization here and elsewhere in the United States has served primarily Hmong clients, focusing on youth and families, employment issues, English education, cultural training, and health.[32]

In 1979, a group of progressive Hmong refugee women founded an organization in St. Paul whose mission would differ from that of Lao Family. Gaoly Yang, the first executive director of Women's Association of Hmong and Lao (WAHL), discusses why WAHL was created even though there was already a Hmong organization: "We wanted a woman director and [to] create programs that empower women. Handcrafts were something that women were interested in expanding and market[ing], and [there were] other things they wanted to learn that were not priorities for the men." The organization focused on women, but leaders were also committed to their Lao identity; still, until WAHL disbanded in 2006, its leaders debated the relevance of the group's name to Hmong American women.[33]

In Minneapolis, another women's organization, Association for the Advancement of Hmong Women in Minnesota (AAHWM), was started around the same time as WAHL to address similar issues in the west metro. One of its cofounders, May Ia Lee, remembers how and why AAHWM was formed:

> At the time, I felt that Hmong women didn't have much peace and many had been abused by their spouses. We wanted to have equal rights, education opportunities, and [a] support system as well as support in building good relationships with our spouses. . . . Hmong women needed the support. We wanted to elevate women's status. So, Mrs. Lee Tou and I started to brainstorm about it. I don't know how we did it. We didn't have much knowledge. But we were able to talk to other supportive people in the larger community who guided us. It was me, Mrs. Lee Tou, Mrs. Ying, just a few of us. Mrs. Tou Fu. Oh, also Mrs. Cher Tha and My Xiong. My was very active just a little after we started.

Today AAHWM is located in St. Paul and continues to provide basic support to Hmong families. However, like some other ethnic-based organizations, it is plagued with financial difficulties.[34]

These first few ethnic organizations have been followed by many others. Most are small and narrowly focused, serving a specific clan or age group. One of the most prominent is Hmong American Partnership (HAP), established in 1990 by community leaders interested in drawing on the strengths of both Hmong and American culture. Since its establishment, HAP has grown from a small community-based organization focused on basic refugee resettlement issues to an established provider of comprehensive, culturally appropriate social services. Among its offerings are

HAP building on Arcade Street, St. Paul, 2007. The Hmong American Center represents hard work and dedication: financial support for construction came from public and private sources, making it a true investment in the Hmong American community. Its banquet room has been the site of many private and community events.

English classes, computer training, youth activities, parental support, job placement, and volunteer opportunities. After moving from site to site throughout the 1990s, HAP purchased an old YMCA building on the east side of St. Paul in 2001. In 2006, HAP opened its doors to the community in this new location.[35]

Most community organizations emphasize cultural preservation as well as provide opportunities for integration. Operating in a different vein, the Hmong Cultural Center's Resource Center in St. Paul maintains a collection with both a community and a scholarly focus. The center houses one of the most—if not the most—comprehensive collections of Hmong studies scholarship in the United States, including books, academic articles, and newspaper clippings related to the Hmong people and the Hmong experience in Minneapolis–St. Paul and across the world. Executive director Txong Pao Lee explains Hmong Cultural Center's role: "It's important for us to provide cultural education to our youth and to provide resources that contribute to cross-cultural understanding between Hmong and non-Hmong people. Too often, there are a lot of problems because people just don't have the opportunity to learn about each other's cultures and traditions." The resource center offers one avenue toward better understanding.[36]

Two other entities make available information about Hmong history and culture. The Hmong Nationality Archives in St. Paul was opened in 1999 as a repository for Hmong-related historical items and out-of-print books. When St. Paul's Concordia University established the Center for Hmong Studies in 2004, the collection moved there. Concordia's initiative was funded with a special gift from a private donor and with support from both Hmong and non-Hmong individuals interested in preserving Hmong history and culture. The center conducts research and publication, promotes teaching and curriculum development, and holds conferences at which scholars can exchange ideas. Its first international conference on Hmong studies, held on March 10–11, 2006, drew scholars from across the United States, Asia, Oceania, and Europe.[37]

A researcher works at the Hmong Resource Center, St. Paul.

Faith-based Organizations

Studies of Hmong refugee resettlement have primarily focused on social service challenges; rarely do they examine faith-based community building. Since the first conversion in 1950, an increasing number both in Laos and elsewhere have joined the Christian church. Organizations were started in Laos, and many enjoyed the support of a church community that goes beyond the clan and kinship system. In the United States, from 1976 to 1978, many small groups of Hmong Christians held worship services in their homes or in their sponsor's churches. After much organizing and with the support of Christian Missionary Alliance (CMA) leaders, a conference was held in California in 1978 to discuss forming a Hmong district organization affiliated with the alliance. At the time, there were 1,525 Hmong Christians in the United States. In the following year, five Hmong CMA churches were established around the country: in Texas on March 4, in Minnesota on March 25, in Colorado and California on April 29, and in Utah on May 25.[38]

The St. Paul Hmong Alliance Church (SPHAC) had its roots in Liberty Plaza, where, under the leadership of Shoua Chai Kong, three families—a total of eleven people—began weekly prayers in 1976. In 1980, the church was incorporated with the state, and in 1986, SPHAC leaders began a capital campaign to raise funds for the congregation's permanent home. Construction began on a location in Maplewood in 1987, and the new building opened its doors the next year. By 2005, SPHAC membership had expanded to 2,895 people. Today, there are more than two dozen Hmong churches throughout the Twin Cities: seven are CMA; other denominations include Assembly of God, Baptist, Catholic, Lutheran, Mennonite, and Methodist. Although a few own their church buildings, most rent space from mainstream congregations. Today, Hmong ethnic churches provide both religious and social support to many families who do not have extended kinship networks.[39]

Telling Their Own Stories

Long without a widely accepted written script for their language, the Hmong have not actively participated in their recorded or written history. Until missionaries, military personnel, and western scholars began documenting Hmong history and culture during the twentieth century, these traditions were passed down orally from one generation to the next. Lacking written documentation and knowledge of their oral educational practices, many Westerners have mislabeled the Hmong as "uncivilized" or "preliterate."[40]

In Laos, access to literacy began in the 1950s, when a written Hmong language (the Romanized Popular Alphabet system) was developed. Greater exposure in the 1960s, thanks to American involvement, inspired excitement about the written word. As Hmong resettled in the United States and other countries, they began immediately to tell their own stories. One of the first efforts to educate and support members of the local community was the "Association of Hmong in Minnesota" newsletter, which provided information primarily in Hmong and English but occasionally used the Lao language. In May 1985, a group of educators and community leaders established *Haiv Hmoob (Hmong Forum)* magazine as a space for creative writing, research about cultural preservation, and news about Hmong throughout the world. Two community newspapers started during the mid-1990s, *Hmong Ywj Pheej* and *Hmong Tribune,* are no longer in circulation. The two papers that currently provide the community's news are *Hmong Times* and *Hmong Today.* Articles are printed primarily in English, but a few stories are available in Hmong language.[41]

Cultural Practices

Contrary to popular perception, Hmong culture has not been static but, rather, flexible and evolving. Migration, both within Asia and in the West, has inspired tremendous changes in the ways traditions are carried out. Regardless of where they reside, Hmong have preserved some aspects of their culture and its traditions at the same time they have accepted new cultural expressions—not unlike other immigrant groups in America.

New Year Celebrations

In villages and towns throughout China and Southeast Asia, Hmong New Year celebrations have served for generations as a centralized gathering after each harvest. Each family or village prepares feasts and invites relatives and friends to partake. It is a time for courtship, when young men and women dress in their finest costumes, hoping to meet a future spouse. They sing folk songs and "toss balls," not only to woo one another but also to entertain spectators young and old. The celebrations usually take place in December and last one to two weeks. Each celebration commences with a special ceremony to drive away the evil spirits of the past year and to ask for blessings from the ancestors for the coming year. According to Yang Dao, an expert in Hmong culture and the first person of Hmong ethnicity to receive a doctoral degree,

> Depending on the size of each village, Hmong New Year lasts from four to five days to more than ten days. Everyone gathers to share feasts, bless one another, and work together to build a better future for the community. These are times for Hmong people to remember and respect Hmong religious and cultural practices. That is why regardless of what country, state, or city Hmong people reside in, we continue to celebrate our New Year. . . . Because each family has prepared a pig, each village enjoys ongoing feasts for four to five days. People from all walks of life who come to

Hmong villages are invited to eat and drink with the villagers.[42]

New Year celebrations have evolved significantly since Hmong have lived in Minnesota and elsewhere. In the early days when there were few families, the New Year was a time for sharing a meal or simply being in the company of other Hmong people. As Dang Her remembers, "We missed our friends and families so much that when we learned about other Hmong families in Minnesota, we immediately tried to contact them. The New Year celebration was quite different from what you see today. Each family contributed some food. It was a potluck. We were all just happy to be with other Hmong families." Ly Vang further describes the evolving celebration: "In 1977, we gathered a lot because we were all still dealing with [the] loss of our own family support. I think 1978 was the bigger New Year celebration; I think there were about twenty-five families. Then we started to move to churches in St. Paul, then the International Institute. The first big New Year was 1983, and 1984 we had the first beauty pageant."[43]

As the number of Hmong Minnesotans increased, the ways in which celebrations were held changed. While individual meals or gatherings based on kinship and clan affiliation are still common components, the growing Hmong population demanded a larger space to host the New Year event. Unlike in California, where outdoor festivities similar to those in Asia take place, the cold midwestern weather requires that the events be held indoors. The availability of large convention centers determined when the Hmong New Year celebration could take place. Furthermore, organizers could not fully conduct certain religious rituals because of regulations governing the sacrifice of animals in public spaces.

While in Asia it is common for different villages to hold

Dang Her stands at the entrance of a New Year celebration held at Harriet Island in St. Paul during the early 1980s. In those days, signs were frequently written in English and in Lao.

their own celebrations and invite others to join them, in Minnesota and other states with large Hmong American populations individual cities have often held their own celebration, considered by some to continue the New Year tradition and by others as a sign of division. This latter perspective was in evidence when in 1998 a large New Year celebration emerged in Minneapolis, scheduled for a few weeks after the St. Paul gathering, which historically has occurred over the weekend following Thanksgiving. The situation is not unique to this state: in California, cities such as Sacramento, Merced, and Fresno all have separate celebrations, while in Wisconsin, cities ranging from Madison to Green Bay, Fond du Lac, and La Crosse hold their own celebrations. Within the city of Milwaukee, two different

New Year celebrations occurred in fall/winter 2006. Several Wisconsin celebrations are held in August and September, when the weather allows for outside activities, which frequently include soccer and volleyball competitions.

Change is visible at all New Year events: many young people no longer wear Hmong costumes, few know how to sing folk songs, and new practices, such as beauty pageants, music, and dance, challenge Hmong traditions. Hmong New Year is a time to rest and enjoy the festivities, yet an economic element has been added in the hundreds of vendors who sell items ranging from imported herbal

Hmong American New Year opening in Minneapolis with Senator Mee Moua (farthest left), New Year committee chair Shong Yang (second from left), Representative Cy Thao (center back), Minneapolis Mayor R. T. Rybak (center right), and Dr. Yang Dao (farthest right)

Women and men tossing balls at Hmong New Year

New Year Festivities Today

Ball tossing provides an opportunity for men and women to meet members of the opposite sex. Some sing folk songs; others simply converse while tossing balls back and forth. Sometimes the tradition is treated as a game: if someone drops the ball, he or she gives up a clothing item, such as coins or a necklace. Although many young people in the United States now use tennis balls, women traditionally folded cloth into a round shape the size of a fist and stitched around the exterior.

Families in America have many choices when dressing for New Year celebrations. While some rise early to prepare their best outfits, others may choose to dress in western-style clothes. Every so often, one sees non–Hmong American friends dressed in Hmong costume as they attend the celebration.

Txong Pao Lee and family

Beauty Pageants

Beauty pageants are not a completely new phenomenon for Hmong Americans: they were introduced during the war years in Laos. However, the pageants in Minnesota have evolved greatly. While it is still very important for contestants to speak the Hmong language, the types of talents they display vary. For example, some play musical instruments; others dance. Both the St. Paul and Minneapolis celebrations host beauty pageants. In the late 1980s, St. Paul held a few contests for men; in Minneapolis, the Prince Charming contest has been an integral part of this festive event.

Beauty Queen crowned at the St. Paul New Year celebration, 2006

Contestants for the Beauty Queen and Prince Charming titles at the Minneapolis Hmong New Year, 2006

Costumes and Jewelry

In Hmong society in Laos, clothing displays an individual's wealth, status, skill, and work ethic. Men and women wear their best clothes for New Year celebrations and weddings. Differences in language and custom distinguish the two Hmong groups: Hmong Der (White Hmong) and Mong Leng (Blue Hmong). Speakers of both dialects understand one another for the most part. The external marker of difference between the two groups was their clothing style; however, today young people wear both styles interchangeably. In addition, transnational travels and imports have resulted in many Hmong Americans wearing the clothing styles of the Hmong in Thailand, China, and Vietnam, which differ from those of the Hmong of Laos. Regardless of which group one belongs to, a Hmong costume is not complete without coins and a silver necklace.

Decorative coins

medicine to travel videos to costumes of all styles and colors. Those with food booths labor to feed the thirty to forty thousand people who participate each year.

New Year celebrations provide a space for artists of all types to display their talents. The variety of music and dances illustrate how Hmong culture has evolved and been enriched by influences from other traditions, whether American popular and hip-hop music and dance styles or Chinese, Bollywood, and Korean dances.

Sports Festivals

Sports have also played a significant role in Hmong American community-building efforts. While the first wave of refugees used soccer as another opportunity to gather, sports festivals have become competitive events that draw

players as well as spectators from around the country and abroad. Between the time the snow melts and when cold weather sets in again, Hmong American soccer tournaments take place somewhere in Minnesota and Wisconsin almost every weekend. Teams traverse state borders to compete, and friends and relatives congregate to enjoy the festivities. The largest sports tournament occurs over the Fourth of July weekend in St. Paul.

Like New Year celebrations, soccer festivals have their roots in early refugees' efforts to bring Hmong community members together. In the early 1980s, the first soccer event was held at Harriet Island in St. Paul, but as the community grew, that space became too small. The tournament moved to several other locations, including Fort Snelling near the international airport, until the City of St. Paul granted permission for it to be held at Como Park, a central location offering easy access for participants. Similar to New Year celebrations, sports tournaments are a fascinating site of economic activities. Vendors selling all kinds of products are stationed in row after row, with food vendors lining one side of the field. Their fare represents the tastes of the

Festive Gathering

The smell of homemade food and the sound of persistently loud noises may seem foreign to those who attend Hmong soccer festivals for the first time. No rain may be visible, but umbrellas pop up everywhere for protection against the hot sunshine. Politician after politician is invited to make speeches at the microphone; their voices compete against blaring music that in turn seeks to drown out the loud gen-  erators running from morning until evening. While sports teams from across the United States compete to win the "trophy" of $5,000, children run across the fields dotted with wrapping papers and Styrofoam containers and parents and grandparents spend time catching up with friends and relatives.

Hmong American community: homemade sausages, tapi-oca dessert, purple sticky rice, papaya salad, and noodles (pho) are all available for purchase.

When one thinks of this summer event, soccer usually comes to mind. However, other sports include volleyball, tennis, kato, spinning tops, and flag football. Until recently, volleyball was the only sport where both men's and women's teams competed. Women's soccer began developing a

Selling Culture

"Camping out" for two days during the sports festival is a worthwhile effort for these two entrepreneurs. Although they work hard to appeal to passersby, they also take time to enjoy a little laughter. Their products, particularly the "traditional" clothes and the handcrafts hanging in the back, are mostly imported from Laos or Thailand. One common product, handcraft—or *paj ntaub* in the Hmong language—embroidered with migration stories emerged from the refugee camps. Women and some men sewed these items, which became commercialized and earned their makers a bit of income when they were sent to countries of resettlement. These products are sold at many grocery stores, gift shops, and farmers' markets.

Two entrepreneurs selling Hmong cultural items

Hmong storycloth

Kato is a game played with rules similar to volley-ball. The goal is to use every part of the body with the exception of the hands to move the kato. Here, a player flips over while kicking the kato, which is made of rattan. Thus far, only men compete in this particular sport, which requires quick reflexes and flexibility.

popular following as girls began to join teams at their schools or on their own. Though not viewed in the same competitive light as men's soccer, women's soccer has drawn players from across the country to compete at this tournament.

Food Preferences

In villages throughout Asia where Hmong people live, rice is the staple food. Their diet is enhanced by a variety of vegetables, fish, meat, and spices. There, food items are usually homegrown and meats fresh and home butchered. Meals are served in a communal style: food is placed in the middle of the table and each person eats from the center with a spoon or fork. Cooking methods in-

Girls play soccer at the 2006 Hmong tournament.

Good Eats

Papaya salad is a favorite food item found at most Hmong gatherings. The chef carefully peels off the skin of a green papaya and grinds the fruit into slender pieces of an inch or two. Depending on the customer's preference, she throws a number of hot peppers into a container. After smashing the peppers, she adds garlic cloves, fresh chili tomatoes, papaya, fish sauce, salt, MSG, and other available items. After mixing the ingredients, she offers a bit of the salad for the customer to taste and then adjusts the seasonings as requested.

Preparing papaya salad at the soccer festival, 2006

Sticky rice is a consistent food offering at Hmong gatherings. Soaked overnight in the juice obtained by draining wild purple rice, sticky rice has a distinct purple hue. It may be served with Hmong-style—sometimes spicy—sausages. Stuffed chicken wings are also popular. In an elaborate process, raw chicken wings are deboned and sautéed. Each wing is carefully stuffed with cellophane noodles, meat, cabbage, carrots, and other seasonings before being deep-fried.

clude stir-frying, steaming, boiling, and roasting over an open fire. Pork fat is used extensively in cooking, and ingredients are usually chopped in uniform pieces. Seasonings are essential; besides salt, Hmong cooking frequently includes hot peppers, ginger, green onions, garlic, cilantro, and lemongrass. Today, other seasonings such as coconut and fish and soy sauce are common.

Life in the United States has inspired enormous dietary changes. Many young Hmong Americans now prefer cereal and milk for breakfast and hamburgers and spaghetti to rice for lunch and dinner. But the one-and-a-half generation—those born abroad but raised in the United States—as well as the original refugees still make food choices reminiscent of those available in their homeland. Homegrown vegetables and meat harvested by hunting were not routinely available in their early years in America.

In time, as entrepreneurs participated in such ventures as farmers markets, Hmong grocery stores, and small farms, access to fresh vegetables and meats increased. Two Hmong-owned butcher shops in South St. Paul offer live chickens, pigs, and cows from which Hmong Minnesotans can select a particular animal for slaughter. A new flea market, located in St. Paul's Frogtown area, makes available fresh produce, fruit, and many other items for their consumption seven days a week.[44]

Religion

Prior to contact with western missionaries, Hmong in Asia were primarily animists who held strong beliefs in spirits and the supernatural world. Although the number of Hmong people who have converted to Christianity has increased since the 1950s—indeed, some estimates show that as many as half the population of Hmong Americans are now Christians—the vast majority worldwide still practice animism and ancestral worship.[45]

A shaman (center) performs a healing ceremony.

Because spirits and the supernatural cannot be seen by human eyes, a shaman or *txiv neeb* makes contact with the spirit world. The shaman is believed to have the power to enter another world to negotiate with evil spirits that cause people to become ill. As a spiritual healer and religious leader, the shaman provides guidance to people during times of crisis. Believers rely on the shaman to heal the body and the soul as well as to prevent illnesses. Both men and women are called to be shamans. A person who receives the call may become very ill; he or she will not recover until the call is accepted. A shaman will be asked to diagnose the illness; if the poor health is judged a sign that the person has been chosen, that individual must accept the responsibility or face the consequence of never recovering.

Clan and extended family members participate in rituals, which are performed in the home rather than in a "worship space." Ceremonies often entail animal sacrifice—frequently chickens and pigs, sometimes cows. In the American context, religious practices have undergone much change because rituals such as animal sacrifice are not allowed. If sacrifice of a large animal such as a cow is required, the ceremony will take place in the home but the cow is killed at a butcher shop or other legal location. Religious freedom in the United States has accommodated the practice of animism, but Hmong Americans have also made adjustments to their traditions as necessary.

Funerals

As a people who have long respected their elders, Hmong Americans, regardless of religious preferences, invest a great deal into ensuring that their family members receive proper funeral services. Funeral practices within animist traditions require a multilayered process of sacred rituals and chants to send the dead to the other world and to provide blessings and guidance to family and friends left behind. This process may take several days depending on the social status of the deceased. The elaborate ceremonies are quite expensive: funeral service costs in the United States may be as high as $30,000 to $40,000. Children of the deceased, in particular sons, are responsible for payment.

Whereas in Laos the corpse is kept in the home of the deceased for a few days, in America the rituals take place in funeral homes, with the accompanying several thousand dollars in rental fees. Services may be postponed for weeks due to the limited number of funeral homes and so that relatives and friends from far away may attend. Immediately following a death, relatives and friends support the family with daily visits. Nightly meals are prepared to feed all the visitors. Family members and guests stay up all night at the ceremony site.

In Laos as well as in the United States, relatives and friends from far and near come to pay their respects. Attendees frequently contribute monetary donations that help offset a significant portion of the total funerary cost. Although Hmong American Christians no longer practice rituals associated with animism and ancestral worship, they hold services that may last the same length of time and incur costs equal to "traditional" funerals. Significant changes are emerging: for example, some Christian ceremonies may be open only until midnight so that guests and family members may go home to rest and return the next morning.

Achievements

During the first three decades that Hmong Americans have resided in the United States, new doors have opened for them. Their achievements in politics, education, business, and the arts have surprised many who knew their subsistence way of life in Asia.

Leadership and Political Activism

Choua Thao and May A Yang held prominent positions during the war years as a nurse and a teacher, respectively. They had some education, and they were wealthy enough to hire others to attend to household chores while they performed their jobs. But despite educational and economic gains for select individuals due largely to the war, very few Hmong women held positions of power.

In this patriarchal culture, decisions regarding community issues traditionally involved primarily men. Women exercised power in situations concerning their immediate and extended family's health and well-being, but their roles were often secondary to male household members, particularly in public spaces. Women rarely participated in community affairs; when they did, they usually provided input to their spouses or adult sons. During their colonization of Laos from 1893 to 1954, the French instituted an administrative hierarchy that provided some leadership positions in Hmong villages; these were held by men, who were more likely to be literate. While military positions provided men with new status as never before, women did not enjoy similar opportunities.

A new kind of leadership—one in which women played some role—arose when Hmong refugees arrived in America. Professionals in various fields emerged as new leaders and served as cultural bridges between the Hmong and their American counterparts. In Minnesota and in other parts of the country with significant Hmong populations, these new leaders frequently did not reflect the social structure of the Hmong in Asia: instead, a younger, literate generation stepped forward.

Hmong Americans have enthusiastically exercised their civic duties. Many, both men and women, serve on local, city, county, and state committees and contribute to making Minnesota a livable and welcoming environment for all people. Although numerous individuals make a difference every day, political activism has manifested itself in several key moments in Hmong American history. Choua Lee's election to the St. Paul School Board in November 1991 encouraged the Hmong American community to build power through the American political process. Her election was significant not only for the entire Hmong American community but specifically for Hmong women. Hmong women have consistently contributed to Hmong society, but only in the United States have they had access to and received support for political participation.

A decade later, attorney Mee Moua successfully ran for the Minnesota Senate as the DFL-endorsed candidate during a special election in January 2002, making her the first individual of Hmong ethnicity to be elected to a state legislature. Senator Moua earned reelection in November 2002

Choua Lee for St. Paul School Board

Vote for Choua Lee

A Fresh Face...
A Needed Perspective

Endorsed by: DFL
Labor (AFL-CIO)
Teachers
Women's Political Caucus
Lao Family Community

Vote Tues, Nov. 5.

Choua Lee made history in 1991 when she ran a successful campaign for the St. Paul School Board. She served one term. As an education advocate, Choua has continued to increase opportunities for St. Paul children.

and 2006. She is a proponent of affordable housing and improving tax policies for low-income families, and she has also fought to protect civil rights and to secure funding for crime victims.

The November 5, 2002, election was memorable for Hmong Americans not only because of Senator Moua's re-election but also because community activist and artist Cy Thao earned election to the Minnesota House of Representatives for District 65A, St. Paul's Frogtown. Unsuccessful as an independent candidate in the previous election, Thao

took 81 percent of the vote as a DFL-endorsed candidate in November 2002.

Hmong Americans have tended to align themselves with DFL candidates as witnessed by their close relationships with the late U.S. representative Bruce Vento and senator Paul Wellstone. Non-Hmong political candidates frequently seek support from Hmong Americans. When Jesse Ventura ran for Minnesota governor in 1998, he visited the Frogtown area and met with Hmong American activists and community leaders. During their campaigns in 2000, congresswoman Betty McCollum and senator Mark Dayton engaged Hmong community leaders; after the election, they retained Hmong Americans on their staffs. A Republican Hmong contingent became visible during the 2002 election. This shift can be explained in many ways, but the strong ties Hmong Americans had established with then

mayor of St. Paul Norm Coleman was a contributing factor. Even after the formerly DFL-endorsed mayor changed political affiliations to become a Republican in 1996, he maintained close relationships with the Hmong community, in particular General Vang Pao and his supporters.

What is it about Minnesota that has enabled Hmong Americans to achieve political success? One factor is the critical mass of voters that exists in geographic locations where Hmong American candidates have been successful. But these triumphs go beyond concentrated voting power: school board member Choua Lee, senator Mee Moua, and representative Cy Thao were supported by many in the broader community. Today's new, younger generation of Hmong leaders represents a shift from the former Hmong social system, where elder male clan leaders served as the voice of authority. However, even amidst growing skills

Hmong American community leader Xang Vang meets with former president George H. W. Bush at a 2002 campaign event for Senator Norm Coleman in Rochester. Xang Vang has long encouraged Hmong people to become active in civic affairs as a means to becoming more American. He has worked with elected officials from both the Republican and Democratic parties, from city councilman Bill Wilson to congressman Bruce Vento to Norm Coleman when he ran for Minnesota governor.

in maneuvering through the American political system, campaign strategies continue to involve the older generation, particularly during election time. One strategy implemented by both Senator Moua and Representative Thao included providing transportation and interpreting support to older Hmong American voters, increasing access to the political process as well as votes for both candidates.

Since Choua Lee's success on the St. Paul School Board in 1992, other Hmong community members have stepped up to the plate: Neal Thao was elected in 1995 and served two terms, and Kazoua Kong-Thao was elected in 2003. In fact, an unprecedented six Hmong Americans sought elected office in St. Paul in 2003: four for city council and two for school board. Although neither won, Bao Vang and Toumoua Lee engaged in a hotly contested battle for Ward One, changing the landscape of Hmong politics as they faced each other rather than mainstream incumbents. Paul Demko wrote, "Bao Vang and Toumoua Lee are just [two] candidates in a freewheeling contest that features at least five legitimate contenders, but their presence has created some unusual discussions and disputes among Hmong citizens." Bao Vang ran on a largely progressive platform, garnered the support of many advocacy and labor groups, and viewed younger Hmong American voters as a primary source of support. Toumoua Lee, on the other hand, courted the business sector and Hmong American Christians and also the heads of the eighteen Hmong clans, traditionally the community's leaders. The other two city council races included Pao Yang, who ran to represent St. Paul's East Side, and Christopher Moua, who challenged Ward Seven incumbent Kathy Lantry. Christopher Moua was the first Hmong American candidate to run as a Republican. Neither Pao Yang nor Christopher Moua was successful in their respective races.[46]

The reelection of both Senator Moua and Representative Thao in 2006 shows that they have earned their constituents' respect. Other candidates of Hmong ethnicity have sought public offices in different parts of the country. One of the most significant outcomes for 2006 was the election of Blong Xiong to the Fresno (California) City Council. Whereas both Senator Moua and Representative Thao represent districts with significant Hmong American populations, Blong Xiong earned a seat in a district whose population is not overwhelmingly Hmong, marking a key milestone in Hmong American politics.

Education

Most of the Hmong refugees who entered the United States had little or no formal education. The first Hmong in Laos to attend school were brothers Toulia, Touby, and Tougeu Lyfoung in the 1930s. After graduation from secondary studies, Touby Lyfoung became an eminent Hmong leader under French colonial rule. His success demonstrated to

Hmong villagers the value of formal education. Those who could afford to send their children to school did so after opportunities—usually for sons—became available in the 1950s. According to cultural expert Yang Dao, in 1939 only eleven Hmong attended high school in the entire country of Laos and by 1971 thirty pursued their studies at universities. Reflecting on his years as a student in France, he remembers the struggles but also that persistence enabled him to finish his degree. He explains, "Education is very important for the Hmong people because they did not have many opportunities in Laos. It is embedded in our culture to value education. Because Hmong parents mostly did not go to school themselves, most want their children to succeed in this country. Some people have worked very hard to improve their education, and others have worked to support their children to get a good education in this country because education is the foundation for success."[47]

Immediately upon arrival, many Hmong refugees enrolled in English as a second language (ESL) classes. But without adequate educational preparation, many foreign-born Hmong Americans were not able to advance beyond ESL classes and vocational school. As a group, Hmong Americans remain at the bottom of the educational attainment ladder when compared to other Asian Americans and the entire U.S. population. Considering where they began, however, the Hmong population has made significant progress. In 1990, only a small percentage of Hmong Americans had earned post-secondary degrees. Nationally, only 11 percent held high school diplomas and three percent had bachelor's degrees. By 2000, 52.7 percent of Hmong Americans in Minnesota had completed no schooling, but the percentage of high school graduates was up to 24 percent. Close to eight percent had an associate or bachelor's degree, and one percent had obtained a master's degree or higher.[48]

A contradictory situation exists with respect to K-12 educational achievement in the Hmong American community. On one hand, despite living in low-income families with parents who frequently do not possess the English language skills to assist with homework, many Hmong children have excelled in school and attended major American universities and colleges. Each year in Twin Cities high schools, some Hmong American children struggle to graduate at the same time that others are valedictorians. In 2006, the Hmong American graduation rate reached the same level (83 percent) as that of the white population in St. Paul. On the other hand, in 2004 only 49 percent of Hmong American eighth graders passed the basic skills reading test and 47 percent passed in math, compared to 80 percent of white students passing in reading and 66 percent in math.[49]

Recent years have seen a decrease in Hmong American enrollment at public schools in both St. Paul and Minneapolis. In St. Paul in 2005, 30 percent of the district's 41,000 students spoke Hmong as a home language; in Minneapolis, the Hmong student population of 3,000 was approximately eight percent of overall enrollment. The declining number of Hmong American students attending public school in both major cities is due to the

Dia Cha is an associate professor of anthropology and ethnic studies at St. Cloud State University in St. Cloud, Minnesota, where she teaches courses in cultural anthropology, ethnic studies, Southeast Asian communities, Asian American studies, and Hmong studies. She received her doctorate from the University of Colorado–Boulder in 2000. Today she is one of the world's leading authorities on Hmong cultural traditions and folkways.

Zha Blong Xiong received his doctorate from the University of Minnesota. He taught at Iowa State University and then returned to Minnesota and became one of the first Hmong Americans to earn tenure at an American research university. His interest is in youth and families; he has recently conducted research on early childhood education.

availability of charter schools and increasing relocation to the suburbs. Both factors are partially related to dissatisfaction with traditional public schools and to changing economic status that allows families to purchase homes in suburban communities or to simply seek education alternatives for their children. Hmong American community leaders have developed charter schools that focus on academic excellence but that also emphasize Hmong language and culture, including Hmong Open Partnerships in Education (HOPE) Community Academy, Prairie Seeds Academy, Hmong Academy, and New Millennium Academy; the latter two are located in north Minneapolis. No doubt these and other initiatives will continue to inspire educational progress for the Hmong.[50]

Business Development

Hmong Americans have pursued their American dreams in many ways. Like other immigrant groups throughout American history, they have developed and sustained ethnic businesses in their communities. Despite the fact that most arrive in the United States with little or no property or financial backing, Hmong Americans have made entrepreneurship an integral part of their livelihoods. One of the most common methods for starting a business has been for clans or relatives to pool financial resources. By 1996, growth in the number of Hmong businesses inspired leaders to form the Minnesota Hmong Chamber of Commerce to advocate for a competitive environment. Its 150 members represent sectors ranging from accounting to real estate to auto dealerships.[51]

Despite these successes, Hmong Americans have confronted difficulties in establishing and growing profitable businesses. The number of ventures has increased, but most are struggling to remain in operation. Because entrepreneurs commonly pool individual or small-group

An Entrepreneur's Success Story

Shong Yang's story is just one example of entrepreneurial success in the Hmong community. Eighteen-year-old Shong Yang arrived in Los Angeles, California, on April 1, 1980, with his older brother's family. After training in the culinary arts in Michigan, he made his way to Minnesota

in 1985 and worked as a chef in Crystal. Looking to expand his opportunities, he attended National College and graduated with a degree in business administration. In May 1995 he started a home care agency that over time has greatly contributed to the Hmong community. His agency was recognized by the Neighborhood Development Center as Business of the Year in 1997 and selected as the Hmong Chamber of Commerce Business of the Year in 2006.

Shong Yang earns Hmong Chamber of Commerce Business of the Year award, 2006

Lending a Caring Hand

Dr. Yer Moua-Lor is a chiropractor, acupuncturist, and nutritional counselor. The first Hmong American female chiropractor, she has been practicing for eight years at clinics in Minneapolis and St. Paul, including her own Moua-Lor Chiropractic and Acupuncture. A graduate of the University of Minnesota and Northwestern College of Chiropractic, she has lived in the Twin Cities since she came to America in 1980 with her mother and siblings. She hopes that Hmong businesses will continue to grow and have a positive effect on the state of Minnesota.

resources rather than obtaining financing, many find themselves with limited capital soon after starting a business. Additionally, catering to the Hmong American community limits access to other customers and the ability to expand. Just as their predecessors did, Hmong Americans continue to cultivate their entrepreneurial spirit and to pursue successes in the economic mainstream.

Arts and Entertainment

Hmong American artists, musicians, writers, and film producers have emerged as important contributors to Hmong American culture. While film producers such as Lee Moua and musical groups such as Destiny appeal almost exclusively to the Hmong American community, some—including artist Seexeng Lee and writers Mai Neng Moua, Kao Kalia Vang, Ka Vang, and Lee Vang—have successfully reached a larger audience. Through individual and creative approaches, each person uses his or her artistic skills to convey aspects of Hmong history and culture.

An art teacher at Patrick Henry High School in Minneapolis, Seexeng Lee has shown his work in many galleries across the Twin Cities. Mai Neng Moua is best known for her edited volume of contemporary Hmong American writing, *Bamboo Among the Oaks.* Kao Kalia Vang's work has been published in *Water-Stone Review, Satya Magazine,* and *Paj Ntaub Voice,* and her essay "To the Men in My Family Who Love Chickens" won the 2005 Lantern Books Essay Contest. Ka Vang has earned praise for her poetry, short stories, and drama, in particular *From Shadow to Light,* which was performed at Theater Mu and Mixed Blood Theatre in Minneapolis in 2004. Lee Vang's play *Hmong! The CIA's Secret Army* helped to educate many Hmong Americans and others about this tragic period. Hmong Americans will continue to tell their stories in a variety of genres, just as they long have through folktales and storycloths.

Leej Niam Txoj Kev Hlub (Mother's Love) by Seexeng Lee, acrylic on canvas with 24-karat gold, silver, and copper leaf, 2006

A Dramatic Presence

Every immigrant population has a compelling story behind their travels and transitions, but what separates the Hmong experience from the rest is their direct tie as U.S. allies during the Vietnam War. While many Americans understand that the Hmong are refugees from the Vietnam War, few realize the depth of the relationship the Hmong shared with the CIA and the U.S. government. *Hmong! The CIA's Secret Army* is a powerful play that tells the wartime love story of a thirteen-year-old Hmong boy named Meng Thao who was recruited by the CIA to fight the secret wars of Laos. He is separated from his family and his girlfriend, Pa Vang. Caught in a war he does not understand, Meng Thao wants nothing more than to return to his beloved Pa Vang. It is a story of love, family, war, and, ultimately, immigration to St. Paul.

Hmong! The CIA's Secret Army poster; play written by Lee Vang and first adapted to stage by Lee Vang and Jamie Meyer in 1999; also performed in St. Paul in spring 2006.

Challenges

When considering their successes in education, business, and community development, it is evident that the Hmong in Minnesota have made significant progress. The first arrivals worked diligently to pave the way for those who followed them. With chain migration, family reunification, and spousal sponsorship, the Minnesota Hmong community is becoming increasingly diverse. But, like other immigrant groups, the community has faced its share of challenges as well.

Intergenerational Gaps

As with immigrants throughout American history, the Hmong are not immune to intergenerational conflicts. Parents and grandparents who try to hold onto Hmong traditions often find themselves in opposition to their children's cultural preferences. As young people growing up in multicultural America, Hmong Americans have access and are attracted to ways of living that inspire their parents' disapproval. Additionally, many illiterate immigrant parents find themselves relying on their children as bridges to the larger community in order to maneuver through various systems and service institutions. Whereas some children are sympathetic to the challenges their parents face and go out of their way to assist, others view the situation as a burden, one not imposed on other American teenagers. Because Hmong culture places great emphasis on respect for elders, this shift to parents depending on their children has fractured many parent-child relationships. Further, a lack of interest in Hmong traditions may mean that children and their parents have little in common. Many young people attend funerals and New Year celebrations without appreciating their significance in Hmong society, for example.

While many in the immigrant generation continue to promote the preservation of Hmong language and culture, second-generation Hmong Americans respond with varying levels of interest. One segment expands its literacy skills as a way to maintain the Hmong language, usually within the contexts of churches and community-based organizations. Some enroll in Hmong writing and history classes at the few American colleges and universities that offer them. On the other hand, many young Hmong Americans speak little or no Hmong and do not see a need for developing these skills in today's society.

Standard of Living

Although some Hmong individuals have achieved significant economic success, overall Hmong Americans remain the most impoverished Asian American group in the nation. Such factors as large family size and limited formal education force many to stay in jobs that offer little or no opportunities for advancement, thus perpetuating a cycle of poverty despite their hard work. According to the 2005 American Community Survey, 32.7 percent of the 188,900 enumerated Hmong Americans had income below the poverty level compared to 10.2 percent in the general U.S. population. Hmong households had a median income of $39,225 compared to $46,242 for the general population.[52]

Although the health and well-being of Hmong Americans is significantly better in the United States than it was in refugee camps or in Laos prior to migration, this high level of poverty suggests that it may take some time to improve their socio-economic status. Better educational opportunities will contribute positively to employment choices and thus the standard of living enjoyed by one-

and-a-half and second-generation Hmong Americans. However, young Hmong Americans are not immune to the materialistic aspects of American culture and may not be able to support themselves in ways that their parents could with fewer means.

Gender Roles

Gender roles among the Hmong have been well defined. At the family level, the authority resides with the male head of household. Although women contribute to decisions affecting the family, they do not have the power to "govern" a family or, more specifically, a group of families from the same clan. The group leader, or *tug coj noj coj haus,* is always a male member. When daughters marry, they become members of their husband's household and are considered outsiders of their original families. Sons are part of their father's family; thus, they inherit family properties or belongings.

Changes in gender roles have generally been viewed in a positive light by Hmong Americans; however, these changes have not been without their challenges. Today's Hmong household is quite different from those of past generations. The wife may be the breadwinner. More and more women are working outside the home or pursuing educational goals. Many educated Hmong American women are choosing to stay single into their thirties and are living by themselves rather than in their parents' homes. Some women have taken on larger community responsibilities that affect their roles in the family. Whereas in Hmong society women tended to play a large part in raising children, more fathers now participate in child rearing. These changes are only the beginning: men and women will continue to define and redefine their roles.

Violence

Print and television media have paid close attention to youth and violence as well as to domestic disputes in the Hmong community. Youth violence emerged in the early to mid-1980s. Forming gangs initially to protect themselves from discrimination and in response to violent acts by young people of other backgrounds, Hmong American youth have themselves become involved in crime-related activities as a part of life in America. Crimes against innocent victims as well as fights with rival groups are frequent, particularly during large gatherings such as New Year celebrations and soccer festivals.

Family violence has also emerged as a high-priority issue, beginning in the mid-1990s when a mother of six killed her children. This type of violence is unfortunately exacerbated due to the nature of the incidents. Rather than seeking alternative responses to problems such as marital infidelity, some have taken situations into their own hands through murder and, often, suicide. While dysfunctional family relationships are certainly a factor, other underlying causes need to be understood in the context of cultural and economic challenges. Cultural expectations compounded by lack of a strong clan or kinship support system mean couples receive little or no assistance in resolving issues, while living with limited financial means and enduring dead-end jobs may place greater pressure on parents and children. Low-wage employment also means that both parents have to work, often different shifts, to make ends meet, enforcing further separation from children and from each other. Meanwhile, some Hmong American men sponsor wives from Laos or Thailand, a practice that contributes to the rise in separations or divorces leading to one-parent households that face further economic challenges.

Racism

Hmong people arrived in the United States during an important time for people of Asian descent. The Immigration and Nationality Act of 1965 opened doors for people outside of Europe to immigrate to the United States, significantly changing American demographics by the 1980s. The ways in which Asian Americans had transformed from the "yellow peril" to the "model minority" affected how Hmong refugees fit into America. As people of Asian descent, Hmong Americans looked like other Asian Americans, but they differed in particular ways from them. Many had to rely on government assistance for economic survival, a reality that alienated them from other Asian Americans, who were ashamed of the Hmong. Further, Hmong culture and traditions are frequently regarded by the larger community as un-American and at times are ridiculed. Lack of education, job skills, and urban living experiences as well as differences in physical appearance may contribute to discrimination at work or taunts in the street. Many Hmong university graduates find it difficult to secure jobs and attribute this to racism. In addition, the immigrant generation's inability to communicate effectively in English is perceived as a lack of commitment to America, despite the fact that a high percentage of the elderly population has become naturalized U.S. citizens.

Identity

When mainstream news media covered Hmong-related events during the mid- to late 1970s, all refugees were lumped into the Southeast Asian or Indochinese categories. If these broad categories were divided up at all, Hmong were primarily placed under the Laotian label, leading to much confusion about the two groups. In Laos, people of

Hmong ethnicity were referred to as *Meo;* in China, they are a subgroup of the "Miao" people, which include all non-Chinese minorities. People of Hmong ethnicity have historically referred to themselves using the term *Hmong.* Hmong in countries of resettlement have also debated—passionately and without reaching consensus—about using the terms *Hmong* for white Hmong and *Mong* for blue Hmong. Traditional dress, some cultural practices, and language dialect distinguish between the two groups. This situation is complicated by national identity adopted in countries of settlement such as Thai Hmong, Lao Hmong, or Hmong American. In truth, Hmong in the twenty-first century have multiple identities; when discussing people of Hmong ethnicity, it is essential to situate them in historical and geographic contexts.

Leadership

Even as mutual assistance agencies have played an integral role in rebuilding Hmong refugee lives in America, they have not been immune to the changing priorities of funders nor to the test of remaining relevant to the evolving Hmong American community. Internal and community politics have increasingly challenged the leadership of these organizations, inspiring investigations into their business practices. The extent to which today's Hmong American community leaders work together to resolve their differences will determine the degree to which community-based organizations remain an important part of their life in America.

Conclusion

American covert operations in Laos during the Vietnam War changed the course of Hmong history forever. U.S. withdrawal from Southeast Asia created a tragic situation

Shong Yang
with daughters
Nkauj Hnub
and Nkauj Hli

but also enabled Hmong to migrate to the United States and other western nations as refugees. In Minnesota and elsewhere, many refugees and their children have achieved success in politics, education, and business, developing a new, vibrant community even as their culture and traditions are evolving in the new land. Their journeys to Minnesota have been accompanied by numerous challenges, however, including poverty, youth violence, family instabilities, and racial and ethnic discrimination. Still, many have worked tirelessly to rebuild and improve their lives and to create a prosperous environment for both their ethnic community and that of Minnesota more broadly.

During the last thirty years, Hmong Americans have engaged in homeland politics at the same time that their civic involvement in American society has evolved enormously.

Participation in the global economy has enabled Hmong Americans to build and sustain transnational ties with relatives in Laos and those in disparate locations throughout the western world. Although a people without a nation of their own, if their brief history in America is any indication, the Hmong will continue to wield social, cultural, economic, and political influence in Minnesota, the United States, and abroad.

Personal Account:
Reflections by Mao Heu Thao

Mao Heu Thao is a Hmong American woman who has played a significant role in transferring information and understanding between Minnesota and refugee camps in Thailand. She and her husband, Toua Thao, arrived in Minnesota from Ban Vinai refugee camp on March 15, 1976, when she was only sixteen years old. Despite the fact that she was surrounded by kind and helpful volunteers, she remembers her feelings of fear and isolation as she faced an unknown future.

Mao works as the Hmong health coordinator for the St. Paul–Ramsey County Department of Health. She formed the Hmong Health Care Professionals Coalition, through which she has taken the lead in providing health promotion through media such as Kev Koom Siab Health Talk Shows and Emergency and Community Health Outreach. Mao helps organize the annual Hmong Health Fair, which brings doctors, nurses, health educators, and other professionals from various metropolitan-area agencies as well as members of the Hmong community to work side by side to address health concerns. In 1992, she worked for six months in Phanat Nikhom, seeking to ensure the well-being of refugees there. Mao was a delegate on the team that assessed the conditions of the Wat Tham Krabok refugees in 2004. She lives with her husband and two children in Savage.

In a personal interview with the author on October 7, 2005, Mao reflected on her migration experience.

From May of 1975 to March 15, 1976, I lived with my husband and family in Ban Vinai refugee camp in Thailand. Just before leaving Ban Vinai, I remember being afraid. I knew we were going to a country

Mao Heu Thao

called America, but I couldn't even imagine what the place would be like—whether it was hot or cold; what would the people look like. I had seen some Americans in Laos and had heard how prosperous America was. But I didn't know anyone who had experienced the country first-hand who could share their experiences with me. One of my greatest fears of leaving the camp to go to America was that I was going to be separated from my parents, aunts and uncles, and brothers and sisters forever. All kinds of thoughts went through my head. What if they got sick or I got sick? What if one of us died? We wouldn't be able to be there for each other at these times. The departure marked a sad and heartbreaking moment in my life, but I closed my eyes and tried to exist from day to day. I didn't want to be trapped in the refugee camp. My dreams were that we would find a safe place to live and work to support ourselves and be free from the hunger and poverty we had experienced in the camp. That was all we hoped for.

When we boarded the bus at Ban Vinai refugee camp, many people from the refugee camp got on the bus with us. But once we got to Bang-kok [International Airport], people began to disperse and went their own ways so that, in the end, we found that we were alone. What was confusing was that all of us from the camp thought we would be going to the same place in America on the same plane, but we found that wasn't the case. At different points along the trip, people we knew started to disappear, and we thought either we were lost or other people were lost, but we kept going.

Toua and I arrived at the international airport in Minneapolis on March 15, 1976. I was wearing a pair of sandals, a light shirt, and [a] skirt. That was all I wore because that was all I had. We felt we looked so odd; we felt so cold. No one had told us how cold it would be. I was so surprised when the extreme cold wind greeted me at the door. I didn't understand until the next day after, when I actually saw snow on the ground. I had seen pictures of snow before, but I had no idea how cold it could be. I was shocked and couldn't believe how something so white and so beautiful could be so cold.

Mr. Jimmies Becky, a representative from Catholic Charities in Winona, met us at the international airport and drove us to Winona. I remember how hungry we were during the long drive. We had not eaten any food on the plane because we did not like it and we did not know how to make our needs known since we could not make ourselves understood. Luckily, when we reached Winona, Mr. Becky guessed our need and took us to eat at a restaurant. I think it was a McDonald's, but I don't remember exactly. By the time we reached the restaurant, I was unable to eat anything because it was so late at night and I was so tired from the trip. And I did not know what to order at the restaurant. So I remember that my poor stomach was growling all night long.

Jim helped to check us into a motel and came back the next morning to pick us up. He took us to some offices. I think we went to a church or maybe the offices of Catholic Charities. My first task was to go through used clothes to see if I could find anything that would fit me. I didn't know then, but now I know that it was a thrift store. I didn't know what to do at the time. I was so thin and little. Wherever I looked, there were humungous-sized clothes. They also smelled strange. There were piles of old shoes. People kept trying to help us by bringing us clothes that might fit, but in my mind I was thinking, "These are all old and used things." I didn't mind that they were old and used, but I didn't understand why the store looked different and only carried old things. What was even more strange was that I didn't know what clothes I should take. I didn't have any money, so I was afraid to pick out anything. The ladies in the store pointed to clothes and shoes and probably told me to go find things, but I didn't understand so I didn't choose anything. I just stood there. Finally, the ladies looked at me and then they would go and bring me various items. I only accepted the ones they brought to me. After we got some clothes, Jim and another person drove us to our new home in America. Our sponsor was the Crucifixion Catholic Church in La Crescent. We met with Father Donald Winkle. We lived with him for a month before moving into our little home across from the church.

While living with Father Winkle, there were a couple of wonderful women who made our beds and cooked for Father, so we ate with him. I was very shy and felt uncomfortable eating with Father because I didn't know much about American foods. It is one thing to get here and to live by yourself and not know what to do. It is another to live with Americans, perfect strangers who I couldn't even communicate with. It was difficult because I didn't know what to do and how to fit in. A major part of this was due to the lack of information and knowledge of America's culture and ways of life. In those first few days, I was really afraid and started to worry that people might not like us because we were not good enough. What a dark awakening! I realized for the first time that my husband and I were the only two people who looked different, and my world turned dark. I was scared, sad, and wondered if we had made the right choice by leaving our families and everything we knew behind. We were so young, and how could we survive in this country with no English, no work experiences, and especially without families? But in the end, we were blessed: the people in La Crescent turned out to be wonderful people. They welcomed and accepted us by opening their hearts, their homes, and sharing their lives with us.

During those first couple of months, Toua followed Father around and Father taught him many things about life in this country as well as practical skills like planting trees and counting money at the church. We are grateful to these wonderful people and will forever be in debt to Father Winkle, Jody, John and the Howe family, Malita K., and the nuns from Crucifixion Catholic Church for rescuing and helping us in our most critical time in this new land. To us, La Crescent is our first home. We still make special trips: visiting the town, checking out the trees Toua personally planted a long time ago. We reminisce about the extraordinary journey we made thirty years ago, and we remember our blessings.

For Further Reading

Chan, Sucheng, ed. *Hmong Means Free: Life in Laos and America.* Philadelphia, PA: Temple University Press, 1994.

Deztner, Dan. *Elder Voices.* Walnut Creek, CA: Altimira Press, 2004.

Duffy, John. *Writing from These Roots: Literacy in a Hmong-American Community.* Honolulu: University of Hawaii Press, 2007.

Faderman, Lillian, with Ghia Xiong. *I Begin My Life All Over: The Hmong and the American Immigrant Experience.* Boston, MA: Beacon Press, 1998.

Fadiman, Anne. *The Spirit Catches You and You Fall Down: A Hmong Child, Her American Doctors, and the Collision of Two Cultures.* New York: Farrar, Straus and Giroux, 1997.

Faruque, Cathleen Jo. *Migration of the Hmong to the Midwestern United States.* Lanham, NY, and Oxford: University Press of America, Inc., 2002.

Hamilton-Merrit, Jane. *Tragic Mountains: The Hmong, the Americans, and the Secret Wars for Laos, 1942–1992.* Bloomington: Indiana University Press, 1993.

Koltyk, Jo Ann. *New Pioneers in the Heartland: Hmong Life in Wisconsin.* Boston, MA: Allyn and Bacon, 1998.

Morrison, Gayle. *Sky Is Falling: An Oral History of the CIA's Evacuation of the Hmong from Laos.* Jefferson, NC, and London: McFarland & Company, Inc., 1999.

Moua, Mai Neng, ed. *Bamboo Among the Oaks: Contemporary Writing by Hmong Americans.* St. Paul: Minnesota Historical Society Press, 2002.

Ranard, Donald A., ed. *The Hmong: An Introduction to their History and Culture.* Washington, DC: Center for Applied Linguistics, 2004.

Notes

1. See Jane Hamilton-Merrit, *Tragic Mountains: The Hmong, the Americans, and the Secret Wars for Laos, 1942–1992* (Bloomington: Indiana University Press, 1993), Sucheng Chan, ed., *Hmong Means Free: Life in Laos and America* (Philadelphia, PA: Temple University Press, 1994), and Roger Warner, *Back Fire: The CIA's Secret War in Laos and Its Link to the Vietnam War* (New York: Simon & Schuster, 1995).

2. *Indochina* is the term the French coined for areas under their colonial rule, which include today's Cambodia, Laos, and Vietnam.

3. Promises made by the U.S. government have been contested during the last three decades because no written documents exist. However, former CIA agents as well as other Americans involved in the operation in Laos have worked alongside Hmong Americans to seek recognition for the role that Hmong people played during the "secret war." See Warner, *Back Fire*, preface.

4. Personal interviews with Yia Lee, Sep 2, 2005, St. Paul, MN, and May A Yang, Jun 24, 2006, St. Paul, MN.

5. Edgar "Pop" Buell was an Indiana farmer who worked for IVS and become the key USAID individual directing distribution of food and supplies as well as education and health services. Personal interviews with Choua Thao, Aug 10, 2005, Minneapolis, MN, and Diana Dick, Oct 15, 2005, Antioch, TN. For a detailed account of the USAID's village health program, refer to Charles Weldon, *Tragedy in Paradise: A Country Doctor at War in Laos* (Bangkok, Thailand: Asia Books, 1999).

6. Personal interview with Gaoly Yang, Sep 14, 2005, St. Paul, MN.

7. Gayle L. Morrison, *Sky Is Falling: An Oral History of the CIA's Evacuation of the Hmong from Laos* (Jefferson, NC, and London: McFarland & Company, Inc., 1999), 9.

8. Hamilton-Merrit, *Tragic Mountains*, 334.

9. Personal interview with Shoua Vang, Oct 3, 2005, Hugo, MN.

10. Personal interviews with Toua Thao, Oct 22, 2005; Mao Vang Lee, Aug 21, 2005; Shong Yang, May 4, 2006; and Tong Vang, Aug 8, 2005; all St. Paul, MN.

11. U.S. Department of Health and Human Services Administration for Children and Families, "Eligibility for Refugee Assistance," http://www.acf.hhs.gov/programs/orr/geninfo/index.htm (accessed Apr 2006). The definition of a "refugee" is outlined in the 1967 United Nations Protocol relating to the Status of Refugees and solidified by the Refugee Act of 1980. *Refugee* is defined as "[Any] person who is outside any country of such person's nationality or, in the case of a person having no nationality, is outside any country in which such person last habitually resided, and who is unable or unwilling to return, and is unable or unwilling to avail himself or herself of the protection of that country because of persecution or a well-founded fear of persecution on account of race, religion, nationality, membership in a particular social group, or political opinion." United Nations High Commissioner for Refugees, *Resettlement Handbook* (Geneva, Switzerland: The Commission, 2004).

12. A few families resettled in Argentina and Germany in the late 1970s. About 1,000 went to French Guyana, in South America.

13. Minnesota Department of Public Welfare, "A Demographic and Service Utilization Profile of the Indochinese in Minnesota: A Summary" (St. Paul, MN: The Department, 1977). Available at Minnesota Historical Society, State Archives, Public Welfare Department Refugee Program Office, Volume 2.

14. Personal interview with Ly Vang, Aug 18, 2005, Minneapolis, MN. She and her husband initially resettled in Madison, IA.

15. Personal interview with May Ia Lee, Oct 24, 2005, Brooklyn Park, MN.

16. Personal interview with Kathleen Vallenga, Jan 6, 2006, St. Paul, MN.

17. A lawsuit regarding concentration of poverty in the mid-1990s resulted in the public housing complexes of Sumner Field and Olson being demolished and their residents dispersed throughout the Twin Cities. Some former residents have been given the opportunity to live in a new mixed-income development on these sites. Hmong National Development, Inc., and Hmong Cultural and Resource Center, *Hmong 2000 Census Publication: Data and Analysis* (Washington, DC: Hmong National Development, Inc., and Hmong Cultural and Resource Center, 2004).

18. Mao Vang Lee, Tong Vang, and Gaoly Yang interviews; personal interview with Mai Yer Her, Jan 2, 2006, St. Paul, MN.

19. The St. Paul Foundation, "Refugee Newsletter" 2.1 (St. Paul, MN: Apr 10, 1983). Documents found at the Immigration History Research Center, Refugee Studies Collection, University of Minnesota, Minneapolis.

20. Author's tabulations based on research and community observations.

21. Donald A. Ranard, ed., *The Hmong: An Introduction to Their History and Culture* (Washington, DC: Center for Applied Linguistics, 2004), 9.

22. May A Yang interview.

23. At the national level, steps were taken to direct Hmong refugees to such states as Arkansas with the expectation that they would practice farming. Lacking capital, however, many relocated to urban areas with larger Hmong populations. Office of Refugee Resettlement/U.S. Department of Health and Human Services, *Hmong Resettlement Study* (Washington, DC: U.S. Department of Health and Human Services, 1984).

24. Personal interview with Xang Vang, Oct 11, 2005, St. Paul, MN.

25. The St. Paul Foundation, "Refugee Newsletter" 2.9 (St. Paul, MN: Sep 10, 1983). Tong Vang interview.

26. The author's father was one of the participants; her family lived on the farm for one year. Minnesota Historical Society, State Archives, Public Welfare Department Refugee Program Office, Vol. 2. Some of the background information is based on data the author gathered in preparing a report on agricultural projects for Hmong Americans for the Minnesota Food Association in 2005, titled "An Overview of Past Farming Efforts and Current Agricultural Practices in the Hmong American Community."

27. During the last five years, many Hmong Americans have moved to the southern states of Arkansas, Missouri, North Carolina, and Oklahoma to purchase farms, in particular chicken and breeder. Most sell their homes and use their savings from the last few decades

as down payments. Their success rate has been mixed.

28. Ranard, *The Hmong: An Introduction*. The recognized eighteen clans are Cha (Chang), Cheng, Chu, Fang, Hang, Her (Heu), Khang, Kong, Kue, Lee (Ly), Lor (Lo), Moua, Pha (Phang), Thao, Vang, Vue, Xiong, and Yang.

29. Donald A. Ranard, "Mutual Assistance Associations: Refugee Self-Help Groups Play Key Role," *In America: Perspectives on Refugee Resettlement* 8 (Washington, DC: Refugee Service Center, Center for Applied Linguistics/Bureau of Refugee Programs of the U.S. Department of State, 1990).

30. A letter dated August 2, 1977, from Hmong community leaders Tou Fu Vang and Leng Vang to the Minnesota Department of Human Rights Commissioner highlights the organization's needs and outlines the various struggles refugees were facing. Minnesota Historical Society, State Archives, Public Welfare Department Refugee Program Office, Vol. 2.

31. Personal interview with Dang Her, Oct 29, 2005, Maple Grove, MN; Tong Vang interview. Quote from report describing the history of the Association of Hmong in Minnesota: Minnesota Historical Society, State Archives, Public Welfare Department Refugee Program Office, Vol. 2.

32. Minnesota Historical Society, State Archives, Public Welfare Department Refugee Program Office, Vol. 2, and interviews with Dang Her, Tong Vang, and Xang Vang. Dang Her and Tong Vang were cofounders of the Hmong Association, and Xang Vang was its executive director when the organization became Lao Family Community of Minnesota. Lao Family Community of Minnesota, Inc., http://www.laofamily.org (accessed Jun 2006).

33. Gaoly Yang interview.

34. Ly Vang and May Ia Lee interviews.

35. Hmong American Partnership, http://www.hmong.org/ (accessed Jun 2006).

36. Hmong Cultural Center, httt://www.hmongcenter.org (accessed Jul 2006). Personal interview with Txong Pao Lee, May 8, 2006, St. Paul, MN.

37. Center for Hmong Studies/Concordia University–St. Paul, http://www.scp.edu/hmongcenter (accessed Jul 2006).

38. Naolue Taylor Kue, *A Hmong Church History* (Thorton, CO: Hmong CMA District, 2000).

39. St. Paul Hmong Alliance Church, http://www.sphac.org (accessed Jul 2006). Personal interview with St. Paul Hmong Alliance Church senior pastor Dr. Nha Long Yang, Aug 10, 2006, Maplewood, MN.

40. Several writing systems had been developed during the nineteenth and early twentieth centuries, but none reached broad acceptance. Haiv Hmoob, Inc., *Hmong Forum* (Minneapolis, MN: 1990). See John M. Duffy, *Writing from These Roots: Literacy in a Hmong-American Community* (Honolulu: University of Hawaii Press, 2007), and Ranard, *The Hmong: An Introduction*.

41. Refugee Studies Center Collection, Series 3, Box 2, Immigration History and Research Center–University of Minnesota. Although not complete, the collection includes original copies of the newsletters and magazines.

42. Yang Dao, "Keeb Kwm Tsiab Peb Caug (Purpose of New Year Celebrations)," *Haiv Hmoob* 1.2 (St. Paul: Nov 1985): 38–43. Translation by author.

43. Dang Her and Ly Vang interviews.

44. *One-and-a-half* refers to immigrant children born abroad but raised in the United States. Usually, these children

have established some foundation in their native language.

45. Ranard, *The Hmong: An Introduction*, 14.

46. Wameng Moua, *Hmong Today,* Nov 17, 2006, 1. Paul Demko, "A Face-Lift for the St. Paul City Council: Primaries Could Mean a Stronger, Tougher Lineup," *City Pages,* Sep 3, 2003, www.citypages.com (accessed Aug 23, 2006). Xa Moua, "Christopher Moua (Rep.) Runs for St. Paul City Council," *Hmong Times,* Jun 16, 2003.

47. Gary Yia Lee, "Minority Policies and the Hmong in Laos," http://www.hmongnet.org/hmong-au/hmong82a.htm (accessed Nov 12, 2006). Personal interview with Dr. Yang Dao, Jan 12, 2006, Brooklyn Park, MN.

48. Kou Yang and Mark E. Pfeifer, "Profile of Hmong Educational Attainment," in *Hmong 2000 Census,* 21, 22.

49. Aron Kahn, "Hmong Graduation Rate Same as Whites: Student Progress to Be Featured at National Conference," *St. Paul Pioneer Press,* Mar 17, 2006, B7. Va-Megn Thoj, "Hmong Achievement Gap Has Grave Consequences," *St. Paul Pioneer Press,* Oct 24, 2004, B8.

50. Minneapolis Public Schools, http://www.mpls.k12.mn.us/ (accessed Jul 26, 2007). See Hmong Open Partnerships in Education (HOPE) Community Academy, http:www.hope-school.org (accessed Jul 2006); Prairie Seeds Academy, http:www.prairieseedsacademy.org (accessed Jul 2006); and New Millennium Academy. HOPE Community Academy opened in 2000; Prairie Seeds Academy and New Millennium Academy opened in 2004. In 2007, two other Hmong-focused charter schools opened: Long Cheng Academy and Community School of Excellence.

51. Federal Reserve Bank of Chicago and Minneapolis, "Credit Availability in the Minneapolis–St. Paul Hmong Community," 2002. Minnesota Hmong Chamber of Commerce, http://www.hmong-chamber.com (accessed Jul 18, 2006).

52. Hmong Cultural Center, http://hmongstudies.org/HmongProfile2005ACS.pdf (accessed Mar 2007).

Notes to Sidebars

1. Mobile Public Information Unit, "Newsletter" 9 (Thailand, Jan 1993).

2. Personal interview with May Ia Lee, Oct 24, 2005, Brooklyn Center, MN.

3. Personal interview with Shoua Moua and Dang Her, Oct 29, 2005, Maple Grove, MN.

4. Personal interview with Bauz L. Nengchu, May 10, 2006, St. Paul, MN.

5. Hmong National Development, Inc. All statistics are from the Minnesota Planning State Demographic Center, available at http://www.mnplan.state.mn.us/demography/DownloadFiles/Asian2000/Asian2000Data.zip (accessed Jun 2006).

6. Wameng Moua, *Hmong Today,* Nov 17, 2006, 1.

Index

Page numbers in *italic* refer to pictures and captions.
Page numbers such as "85n42" refer to information found in Notes.

Picture Credits

May A Yang—pages x, 15 (bottom), 19 (bottom)

Shia Yang—pages 3, 45 (bottom), 46, 47, 48 (top), 50 (bottom)

Diana Dick—page 5

Linda Yang—page 15 (top)

Immigration History Research Center—page 16

Dang Her and Shoua Moua—pages 18, 19 (top), 42

Bauz L. Nengchu—page 21 (top)

Lyda Vang and Yee Her—page 21 (bottom)

CartoGraphics, Inc., Minneapolis—page 22

Shoua Moua—page 25

May A Yang and Tong Vang—pages 27 (top and bottom), 28, 29

Therese Scheller—page 30

Xang Vang, Dang Her, and Choua Thao—page 33

Brian Gardner—pages 34, 36, 37

Shong Yang—pages 43, 65 (top), 75

Hmong Times—pages 44 (top), 45 (top), 50 (top)

Txong Pao Lee—page 44 (bottom)

Shia Yang and *Hmong Times*—page 48 (bottom)

Chia Youyee Vang—pages 49 (top), 51, 52

Photograph by Eric Mortenson—page 49 (bottom)

Wing Young Huie—page 55

Minnesota Historical Society—page 57

Mee Moua—page 58

Cy Thao—page 59

Xang Vang—page 60

Dia Cha—page 63 (top)

Zha Blong Xiong—page 63 (bottom)

Dr. Yer Moua-Lor—page 65 (bottom)

Photograph by Nikki Yang—page 67

Center for Hmong Arts and Talent—page 68

Mao Heu Thao—page 77

Acknowledgments

For the first time, Hmong people are actively participating in the documentation and writing of our collective history. I am grateful for the opportunity to write the story of the Hmong in Minnesota: this history is also my personal history. As part of my dissertation on this subject in the Department of American Studies at the University of Minnesota, which I completed in December 2006, I conducted extensive research at the Immigration History Research Center (IHRC) and in the Minnesota State Archives and I interviewed nearly two dozen Hmong Americans about their resettlement experiences.

Many people contributed to making this book possible. First, I thank my adviser, Dr. Jennifer Pierce, and members of my dissertation committee for their support and guidance during the last two years: Dr. Rod Ferguson, Dr. Erika Lee, and Dr. Helga Leitner. I especially thank Erika Lee and former IHRC assistant director Joel Wurl for the opportunity to examine the International Institute of Minnesota's resettlement materials. IHRC staff member Daniel Necas also provided much research support. I am deeply indebted to the men and women who shared their life experiences with me, some of whom are quoted in this book, and the many community members who graciously provided photographs and other materials. These personal contributions enriched the narrative beyond measure. Thank you to Shannon Pennefeather for her thorough editing of the manuscript and enthusiasm about the project. Dr. Gary Yia Lee's careful review has greatly strengthened this book. My uncle Tong Vang, one of the first Hmong refugees to come to Minnesota, deserves special appreciation for directing me to the many people whose voices are heard in these pages. Finally, thank you to my husband Tong Yang not only for his encouragement and patience but also for his feedback on the many versions this story took.

Minnesotans can trace their families and their state's heritage to a multitude of ethnic groups. *The People of Minnesota* series tells each group's story in a compact, handsomely illustrated, and accessible paperback. Readers will learn about the group's accomplishments, ethnic organizations, settlement patterns, and occupations. Each book includes a personal story of one person or family, told through a diary, a letter, or an oral history.

In his introduction to the series, Bill Holm reminds us why these stories are as important as ever: "To be ethnic, somehow, is to be human. Neither can we escape it, nor should we want to. You cannot interest yourself in the lives of your neighbors if you don't take sufficient interest in your own."

This series is based on the critically acclaimed book *They Chose Minnesota: A Survey of the State's Ethnic Groups* (Minnesota Historical Society Press). The volumes in *The People of Minnesota* bring each group's story up to date and add dozens of photographs to inform and enhance the telling.

Books in the series include *Irish in Minnesota, Jews in Minnesota, Norwegians in Minnesota, African Americans in Minnesota,* and *Germans in Minnesota.*

Bill Holm is the grandson of four Icelandic immigrants to Minneota, Minnesota, where he still lives. He is the author of eight books including *Eccentric Island: Travels Real and Imaginary* and *Coming Home Crazy.* When he is not practicing the piano or on the road circuit-riding for literature, he teaches at Southwest State University in Marshall, Minnesota.

About the Author

Chia Youyee Vang was born in Laos and as a child escaped with her family to the United States in 1980. An assistant professor of history at the University of Wisconsin–Milwaukee, she specializes in the study of Hmong migration and community-building efforts.